POLITICAL AND MILITARY SOCIOLOGY

This special edition of *Political and Military Sociology: An Annual Review* encompasses a full range of coverage on the European refugee crisis. Contributions include a focus on the characteristics and motivations of modern-day migrants, an analysis of the inconsistent standards displayed by the European Union, and the militarization happening across parts of Europe in response.

The volume leads with a discussion on the identity of the refugees: who are they and what are their reasons for leaving their homelands? Following chapters cover the response across Europe in countries including Serbia, Greece, Turkey, and Italy. The penultimate chapter examines the European Union's inadequate response to the unfolding crisis, and the book concludes with a central analysis of the agreements between the EU and transit countries with remarks on the unintended consequences that have emerged.

Taken together, the chapters provide an important and timely study of the still unfolding migration crisis. Beyond the sensationalist media coverage, contributing authors bring to the fore expert knowledge and objective analysis on the treatment of refugees and ultimately contribute to the greater goal of policy relevance and fairer outcomes.

Karthika Sasikumar is Associate Professor in the Department of Political Science at San Jose State University. She has done postdoctoral work at the University of British Columbia and Harvard University. Her research interests are in international security, national identity, and immigration. Her articles have appeared in *Mediterranean Quarterly*, *Review of International Studies*, and *Place Branding and Public Diplomacy*.

Danijela Dudley is Assistant Professor in the Department of Political Science at San Jose State University. She received her Ph.D. in political science from the University of California, Riverside. Her research focuses on civil–military relations, institution building in transitioning societies, the influence of international integration on democratization processes, and European politics.

Political and Military Sociology
Series Editors:
Neovi M. Karakatsanis, *Indiana University South Bend*
Jonathan Swarts, *Purdue University Northwest*

Book Review Editor
Jonathan Swarts, *Purdue University Northwest*

Board of Associate Editors

Sergei Baburkin, *Yaroslavl State Pedagogical University*; **Amir Bar-Or,** *Kinneret College on the Sea of Galilee*; **Robert Benford,** *University of South Florida*; **Hans Born,** *Geneva Centre for the Democratic Control of Armed Forces (DCAF)*; **Clem Brooks,** *Indiana University*; **Michael Conniff,** *San José State University*; **Gebretsadkan Gebretensae,** *Center for Policy Research and Dialogue, Addis Ababa*; **Metin Heper,** *Bilkent University*; **Nila Kapor-Stanulović,** *University of Novi Sad*; **Savvas Katsikidis,** *University Of Cyprus*; **Anícia Lalá,** *University of Bradford*; **Dominique Maillard,** *Université Paris-Est Créteil Val de Marne*; **David Mares,** *University of California, San Diego*; **Leonardo Morlino,** *LUISS, Rome*; **Riefqi Muna,** *Indonesian Institute of Sciences (P2P-LIPI)*; **David Pion-Berlin,** *University of California, Riverside*; **Karthika Sasikumar,** *San José State University*; **Robert K. Schaeffer,** *Kansas State University*; **Riaz Ahmed Shaikh,** *Institute of Business and Technology (BIZTEK), Karachi*; **Henning Sørensen,** *Institute for Sociological Research*; **Marybeth Peterson Ulrich,** *U.S. Army War College*; **Laurence Whitehead,** *Nuffield College, University of Oxford*; **Jerzy Wiatr,** *University of Warsaw*; **Daniel Zirker,** *University of Waikato*; **Marian Zulean,** *University of Bucharest*

POLITICAL AND MILITARY SOCIOLOGY

The European Refugee Crisis

AN ANNUAL REVIEW, VOLUME 45

*Edited by Karthika Sasikumar
and Danijela Dudley*

NEW YORK AND LONDON

First published 2019
by Routledge
711 Third Avenue, New York, NY 10017

and by Routledge
2 Park Square, Milton Park, Abingdon, Oxon, OX14 4RN

Routledge is an imprint of the Taylor & Francis Group, an informa business

© 2019 Taylor & Francis

The right of Karthika Sasikumar and Danijela Dudley to be identified as the authors of the editorial material, and of the authors for their individual chapters, has been asserted in accordance with sections 77 and 78 of the Copyright, Designs and Patents Act 1988.

All rights reserved. No part of this book may be reprinted or reproduced or utilized in any form or by any electronic, mechanical, or other means, now known or hereafter invented, including photocopying and recording, or in any information storage or retrieval system, without permission in writing from the publishers.

Trademark notice: Product or corporate names may be trademarks or registered trademarks, and are used only for identification and explanation without intent to infringe.

Library of Congress Cataloging-in-Publication Data
A catalog record for this title has been requested

ISBN: 978-1-138-59173-8 (hbk)
ISBN: 978-1-138-59174-5 (pbk)
ISBN: 978-0-429-46310-5 (ebk)

Typeset in Bembo
by Apex CoVantage, LLC

CONTENTS

List of Illustrations vii
Notes on Contributors viii

    Introduction 1
    Danijela Dudley and Karthika Sasikumar

1 Who Are the Refugees? A Demographic Analysis 4
    Petar Vrgović and Nila Kapor-Stanulović

2 Serbia and the Migration Crisis: The Power of Framing 18
    Karthika Sasikumar

3 From Ambiguous Refugees to Potential Citizens:
    Turkey's Domestic and International Challenges and
    Its Syrians 36
    Sultan Tepe and Anahit Gomtsian

4 The Ex-Yugoslav States and the 2015 Refugee/Migrant
    Crisis: Victims or Opportunists? 54
    Filip Kovačević

5 Policing the Mediterranean: The Use of Naval Forces in
    Immigration Enforcement 71
    Jonathan Swarts

6 Italy and the Refugee Crisis: The Humanitarian Dilemma 91
   Francesca Longo

7 Challenged Integration: Europe's Refugee Crisis 106
   Danijela Dudley

8 From Technologies of Control to "Facebook Refugees":
   The Unintended Consequences of the EU-Turkey
   Agreement on the Refugee Crisis in Greece 122
   Neovi M. Karakatsanis

ILLUSTRATIONS

Figures

1.1	Trend of Global Displacement and Proportion Displacement, 1996–2015	8
1.2	Major Refugee-Hosting Countries at the Start and End of 2015	10
1.3	Major Source Countries of Refugees at the Start and End of Year 2015	10
1.4	The Flow of Refugees to Other Countries	11
1.5	Dominant Migrant Routes and Number of Illegal Border Crossings	13
6.1	Asylum Applications (non-EU) in the EU-28 Member States, 2005–15 (thousands)	93
6.2	Number of (non-EU) Asylum Seekers in the EU and EFTA Member States, 2014 and 2015 (Thousands of First Time Applicants)	94
6.3	Trend of Migrant Arrivals in Italy	95
8.1	A view of the Vial Refugee Camp in Chios, Greece	131
8.2	A view of the Vial Refugee Camp in Chios, Greece	132

Tables

5.1	Irregular Arrivals to Europe	81
5.2	Arrivals to Greece, 2016	85

CONTRIBUTORS

Danijela Dudley is Assistant Professor in the Department of Political Science at San Jose State University. She received her Ph.D. in political science from the University of California, Riverside. Her research focuses on civil–military relations, institution building in transitioning societies, the influence of international integration on democratization processes, and European politics.

Anahit Gomtsian is a Ph.D. candidate in the Department of Political Science at the University of Illinois at Chicago and a lecturer in politics at Lake Forest College. Her research on urbanization and tourism in the American West appears in *Cities, Sagebrush, and Solitude: Urbanization and Cultural Conflict in the Great Basin* (2015). Her current research focuses on the comparative analysis of refugee admission and integration at state and local levels.

Nila Kapor-Stanulović, the first recipient of the APA International Humanitarian Award, is Professor at the University of Novi Sad and the University of Donja Gorica. As a psychosocial rehabilitation program officer at UNICEF Belgrade, she was responsible for programs for the psychosocial recovery of children affected by armed conflict in Yugoslavia and Bosnia. Since 1995, she has been a consultant to the UNICEF offices in Armenia, Azerbaijan, and Georgia.

Neovi M. Karakatsanis is Professor of Political Science at Indiana University South Bend. She is the co-author of *American Foreign Policy Towards the Colonels' Greece* (Palgrave Macmillan, 2018). Her work has also appeared in *Armed Forces and Society*, the *Journal of Balkan and Near Eastern Studies*, *Democratization*, and *Mediterranean Quarterly*.

Filip Kovačević is the author of several books, including *Liberating Oedipus? Psychoanalysis as Critical Theory* (2007), and dozens of academic articles and magazine and newspaper columns on geopolitics and critical theory. He is on leave from the University of Montenegro and currently teaches at the University of San Francisco.

Francesca Longo is Professor of Political Science and Jean Monnet Professor of European Union Public Policies at the University of Catania. Her research interests are EU migration policy, EU policy against organized crime, and the security policy of the EU. She is the convenor of the Standing Group on Organised Crime—European Consortium for Political Research, a member of the academic board of the *Rivista Italiana di Scienza Politica*, and vice president of the steering committee of the Italian Political Science Association.

Karthika Sasikumar is Associate Professor of Political Science at San Jose State University. She has done postdoctoral work at the University of British Columbia and Harvard University. Her research interests are in international security, national identity, and immigration. Her articles have appeared in *Mediterranean Quarterly*, *Review of International Studies*, and *Place Branding and Public Diplomacy*.

Jonathan Swarts is Professor of Political Science at Purdue University Northwest. He is the co-author of *American Foreign Policy Towards the Colonels' Greece* (Palgrave Macmillan, 2018) and the author of *Constructing Neoliberalism: Economic Transformation in Anglo-American Democracies* (2013).

Sultan Tepe is Associate Professor of Political Science at the University of Illinois at Chicago. She is the author of *Transformative Forces of Religion and the City: The Emergence of American Islam* and *Beyond Sacred and Secular: the Politics of Religion in Israel and Turkey* (2008). Her most recent article, "Contesting Political Theologies of Islam and Democracy in Turkey," appeared in the *Journal of Religious and Political Practice* in 2016. Her current research focuses on transnational movements and democratic rights.

Petar Vrgović is Assistant Professor in the Faculty of Technical Sciences, University of Novi Sad. His main research focus is on business communication and human aspects of innovation. He is also interested in topics that deal with developing countries and undeveloped regions generally.

INTRODUCTION

Danijela Dudley
SAN JOSE STATE UNIVERSITY

Karthika Sasikumar
SAN JOSE STATE UNIVERSITY

It is often said that the first casualty of war is truth. Similarly, the first casualty of a massive refugee crisis is objective and rational analysis. In an age of continuous media coverage, there has been a deluge of information and opinion on the mass migration from the Middle East and other countries in 2015 and 2016. However, what is lacking is serious research that moves beyond the sensational headlines. This special issue of *Political and Military Sociology: An Annual Review* brings together scholars from several countries to analyze the causes and effects of this mass movement of refugees to Europe.

The editors of this issue strove to include scholars with diverse perspectives and to represent viewpoints from different countries. Their goal was to provide a comprehensive view of the refugee crisis in one volume. Thus, the contributions of the various authors run the gamut—from a summary of the characteristics of the migrants themselves, to a study of the inconsistent principles of the European Union (EU); from studies of single countries such as Serbia and Turkey, to analyzes of militarization across Europe.

The first contribution to the volume, by Petar Vrgović and Nila Kapor-Stanulović, focuses on the question: Who are the refugees? By bringing together data from different sources, this piece lays the foundation for the volume. The authors argue that, contrary to popular perceptions, a quest for better economic opportunities is not the primary motivation for migrants to leave their homelands. Instead, decisions to migrate are better explained through a combination of push and pull factors in both the country of origin and the country of destination. The 2015 crisis, they find, was unique as it was produced by a "perfect storm" of a myriad of factors. The escalation of violence in the Middle East served as a necessary push factor for people to embark on a road in search of safe areas. The success of previous migrants who sought refuge in Europe and the development of sophisticated smuggling networks provided additional incentives in the form of pull factors. As a result, the European Union and the countries on the route to it experienced a crisis. Not all were equally well equipped or willing to cope with it.

Other articles in this issue examine the ways in which different countries approached the crisis. As one key country *en route* to the EU, Serbia was faced with a large number of people entering and passing through its territory. According to Karthika Sasikumar, the government chose to approach the issue by framing Serbia as a "transit country." By meeting the immediate needs of the migrant population, the country benefited from improving its reputation internationally. It strove to bring itself closer to membership in the EU. Being less developed than its European neighbors, however, Serbia was unable to provide long-term care for migrants. By presenting itself as a transit country, as opposed to a destination country, Serbia burnished its international reputation while avoiding the costs associated with long-term integration efforts and remaining sensitive to the possibility of public opinion turning against refugees. This strategy, however, backfired when neighboring countries started closing their borders, leaving migrants stranded in Serbia.

Sultan Tepe's article shows that Turkey adopted a similar attitude towards the refugees. Using Giorgio Agamben's concept of "precarity," she reveals that the Turkish response was also based on a refusal to provide long-term solutions for those entering the country in distress and an insistence that the refugees were "guests." She analyzes the political and legal conditions that made such a response possible. Adopting a regional perspective, she expands the analysis to Jordan and Lebanon.

Filip Kovačević expands the analysis of transit countries' responses by examining the extent to which the former Yugoslav states of Croatia, Macedonia, Serbia, and Slovenia used the crisis opportunistically in order to obtain concessions from the EU. The political skills of the countries' leaders, according to the author, determined whether they could convince Western European countries of their commitment to human rights and European values and, consequently, the extent to which they were able to benefit from the crisis. By taking a more humanitarian approach toward the migrants, Serbia and Slovenia were able to extract concessions from the EU in the form of accelerated accession negotiations, favorable attitudes toward the disputed status of Kosovo, or financial assistance. Croatia and the Former Yugoslav Republic of Macedonia, on the other hand, took a more repressive approach, resulting in harm to their international reputations and, in the case of the Croatian government, the loss of political capital at home.

The essays by Jonathan Swarts and Francesca Longo reveal the processes and consequences of militarization. Swarts analyzes the European response to the crisis on its maritime boundaries. This militarization is a result of the view of the refugee crisis as a security threat. Initially, the focus of the EU and, in particular, the countries on the outer edge of the union was on the enforcement of immigration laws and the prevention of illegal migration. As the numbers of migrant arrivals by sea increased, however, European countries began perceiving the crisis as a security challenge that required a more militarized approach. Consequently, both the EU and individual states expanded the role of their militaries to include functions that have traditionally been the responsibility of border patrols and coast guards.

Francesca Longo also examines the consequences of perceiving the migrant crisis as a security challenge. Initially viewing migrants as a security threat, Italy responded by focusing on physically securing its borders, returning migrants to their countries of origin, and reaching agreements with these countries to prevent migrants from leaving. As the tragedies suffered by migrants increased, however, Italy adapted its approach to focus more on the issue of the human security of migrants, as opposed to border security, and consequently began to implement measures oriented more toward humanitarian interventions. While Longo recognizes the increased use of the military in the latter stages, she concludes that such use of the military, in conjunction with law enforcement agencies and non-governmental actors, was appropriate, as it conducted rescue operations and protected the human rights of migrants within the framework of international humanitarian law.

Danijela Dudley's article analyzes the European Union's inadequate response to the refugee crisis and argues that the reaction was consistent with the EU's state of incomplete integration. Although the union has achieved an almost complete integration in some policy areas, in others it still does not have the institutional capacity to act with a unified voice. As one of the more divisive issues within the union because of its close relation to both security concerns and cultural values, asylum and immigration policy has not yet been institutionalized. As a result, the refugee crisis produced not one collective European response, but 28 national responses, leading to the re-introduction of borders within the EU.

The ultimate policy that relieved mass migration pressures on the EU was found not within the EU, but in agreements between the EU and transit countries, such as Turkey. While the EU-Turkey deal led to a significant decrease in the number of migrants reaching the EU, Neovi Karakatsanis argues that the agreement, reached with the goal of balancing the EU's professed commitment to liberal values with public pressure to curtail the flow of refugees, produced a number of unintended consequences. In particular, the author finds that the agreement led to deteriorating conditions in refugee camps, including incidents of violence within the camps, more dangerous journeys for those still determined to reach the EU, worsening perceptions of refugees among the Greek population, as well as the strengthening of smuggling networks.

At the time of writing, the refugee/migrant crisis is still unfolding. In time, as more facts and figures become available, the conclusions presented in this volume may need to be revised. However, scholars should not be deterred from writing about current events. By contributing their expertise to the ongoing heated debate about the treatment of refugees, the authors in this volume strive for policy relevance and fairer outcomes.

1

WHO ARE THE REFUGEES?

A Demographic Analysis

Petar Vrgović

UNIVERSITY OF NOVI SAD

Nila Kapor-Stanulović

UNIVERSITY OF NOVI SAD

Political and Military Sociology: An Annual Review, 2017, Vol. 45: 4–17.

The ongoing migrant crisis has challenged many things that were until now, and especially in the European Union, taken for granted. The causes of a very complex situation in one region of the world have also challenged scholars to try to understand who displaced people are and what their intentions are. This article surveys previous studies on migrants around the world, analyzing the past in order to better understand the present. Secondly, the article compiles available data about the current migrant crisis in order to describe the situation as well as the motivations of those individuals who migrate. The article shows that the present situation is the result of a "perfect storm" for mass migrations, with multiple factors converging both from the territory of origin and the final destination.

Introduction

The year 2015 will, among other things, be remembered as a year in which an unprecedented number of asylum seekers fled to the European Union. This phenomenon was quickly found to be much more than a statistical anomaly and, probably, no less than the biggest social challenge that part of the world had seen in recent years. Experts from a wide range of disciplines became interested in various aspects of this mass migration, some of them trying to understand what made such a large number of people move synchronously toward the same goal, while others tried to define what the goal was in the first place. As the numbers of illegal border crossings and asylum applications went off the charts, Western society struggled to understand what it was facing.

This article aims to describe the basic demographics of the recent migrant crisis, attempting to understand who the migrants are and what they desire to achieve. Certainly, heads can be counted, but aspirations cannot. The authors therefore begin by presenting some previous findings and insights into other migrant crises of a similar nature that, in turn, offer explanations of the current phenomenon.

The Motivation to Migrate to Distant Locations

It is commonly known that it is not easy for most people to leave their homes, belongings, social ties, and communities to start life elsewhere. Therefore, it is important to understand the decision-making process that leads one to migrate. Factors that instigate the move are usually separated into two groups: the relative benefits of moving to a new destination country ("pull factors") and the hardships faced in the sending country ("push factors"). In most cases, non-voluntary migration from one area to another is easily related to the push factors: some form of violent and life-threatening situation, such as war between two states, civil war within one state, or political oppression. People sense they are in direct danger and flee to a safer area, whether to another region of the same country or to a neighboring country.

However, it is more complicated to explain migration to places that are more distant. The usual scenario, "direct danger—minimal movement to a safer area—moving back when the threat is gone," requires minimal resources and little planning and is not sufficient to explain the decisions of people who travel thousands of miles. For such a substantial migration, people need to inform themselves, prepare, and organize. Also, it becomes apparent that individuals who migrate large distances tend to stay abroad and start a new life. In such cases, the public and mass media of the receiving country often question the migrants' motivations, usually claiming that economic motivations dominate. The reasons that migrants themselves put forward for such migrations are then judged as untrue, leading frequently to a decline in sympathy toward migrants among the population of receiving countries.

One example of such a misunderstanding is that of migrants from El Salvador who tried to find a new home in the United States in the late 1970s and early 1980s. During that period, roughly half a million Salvadorans (one person in four) became either an internal or external refugee. Many of them were apprehended as illegal immigrants in the United States (Stanley 1987). At that time, the U.S. government faced a dilemma as to whether these immigrants should be deported or offered special protection. On the one hand, the Reagan administration considered these Central Americans as economic migrants in search for a better life based on the fact that they had passed through Mexico as quickly as possible. On the other hand, the legal staff members of private agencies aiding Central Americans in the United States argued that most of the Salvadorans who came to the United States did so out of fear for their lives because of political violence in their home country. For their part, most of the migrants maintained that they came to the United States reluctantly and planned to return home as soon as it was safe to do so; they also stated that they often suffered considerable hardships in Mexico and, thus, were seeking better temporary shelter. Indeed, it was shown that fleeing political violence was at least an important motivation of Salvadorans who migrated to the United States during the political oppression and civil war in El Salvador: indicators of political violence explained more than half of the variance in Salvadoran apprehensions in the United States (Stanley 1987).

Similarly, Guatemala witnessed an outbreak of political violence, guerrilla attacks, and death squads that started in 1966 and spanned the next two decades. Similar situations were seen in countries such as Honduras, Colombia, Peru, and Nicaragua, where a combination of economic downturns and political oppression conducted by authoritarian regimes drove hundreds of thousands of people out of their homes. Popular models, based on expected wage maximization, failed to explain these instances of migration; people were looking for something more than better wages. Because violence interferes with a person's perception of economic benefits (since the person enjoys less safety and less consumption), economic factors are connected to other factors and should not be seen as dominant in countries that have high levels of violence and conflict. As Morrison concludes, "[M]igration flows are shaped by violence, and the effect of violence on migration tends to increase as the level of violence escalates. Consequently, a narrow focus on economic determinants of migration is inappropriate in high-violence countries" (Morrison 1993: 828).

In addition to these Latin American case studies, a number of studies question the causes of refugee migration on a global scale. For example, Schmeidl identified generalized violence and civil wars with foreign military interventions as variables responsible for producing large refugee populations and prolonged migrations. Thus, while a country's level of economic development was found to influence the total number of refugees, Schmeidl found little evidence of economic and other intervening variables having a direct impact on mass exodus (Schmeidl 1997). Similarly, a large sample of internal and international conflicts between 1964 and 1989 demonstrated that threats to the personal integrity of individuals were of primary importance in forcing people to abandon their homes, especially if the threats were in the form of a civil war or a genocide/politicide. Economic threats and ratios of GNP per capita were not found to have a role in generating refugee movements (Davenport et al. 2003). Finally, Moore and Shellman, who analyzed a significant number of migrations around the world in the period 1952–1995, also concluded that state violence, dissident behavior, civil wars, genocides, and international wars were all factors of forced migration for both internally displaced people and refugees. They therefore concluded that, while institutional democracy and economic factors influenced the size of forced migration, their impact was relatively small; instead, the "push" factor of violence was found to drive the process of non-voluntary migration to a greater extent (Moore and Shellman 2004).

Despite such research findings, it appears that migration to Western Europe in the last few decades took place in a unique context. During the Cold War, asylum seekers from East European communist countries were often accepted by the receiving states since there was clear political and ideological violence aimed at them—they were dissidents with political reputations that needed protection (Neumayer 2005). In the 1970s and 1980s, however, the structure of asylum seekers changed: They were predominantly from third world countries, had less cultural affinity with Europeans, and often arrived through the use of traffickers and false documentation (Hansen and King 2000). While still officially dubbed "asylum seekers" as they tended to apply for asylum, some segments of the public in receiving countries described them as "bogus refugees," branding them as mere economic migrants. This led to calls for restricting the inflow of refugees, resulting in measures aimed at deterrence and deflection, such as the compilation of lists of "safe" countries of origin and "safe" third countries to which the refugees could be returned.

European countries took some time to grapple with the reasons why people seek asylum. Neumayer tried to identify reasons, showing that factors that influence asylum seeking in Western Europe are numerous and interdependent: the economic conditions in the country of origin are statistically significant and substantively important determinants of aggregate numbers of asylum seekers. However, the type of political regime, threats to the personal integrity of the individual, dissident violence, civil/ethnic warfare, and external conflicts were also found to be important factors (Neumayer 2005). Thus, for many refugees it appears that economic factors and violence influence each other, creating a strong "push" for migration. Studies also concluded that migrants are more mobile in larger groups, when a larger number of past asylum seekers exists, when the destination country is geographically closer, and when the possibility of obtaining generous welfare provisions exists. For example, the conflicts in the former Yugoslavia in the 1990s resulted in hundreds of thousands of people fleeing to Western Europe; this should have been seen as a harbinger of the current wave of migration. We note that all of the relevant characteristics were present: the economic decline of the former Yugoslavia, followed by political confrontation that escalated into ethnic violence and ended with foreign intervention; the fact that economic migrants had paved the way previously in smaller numbers; that destination countries were merely hours away by land transport; and that generous welfare benefits existed with relatively easy access to them by migrants.

The Global Refugee Crisis: 2014 and 2015

In recent years, worldwide conflicts have displaced millions of people against their will. The years 2014 and 2015 were particularly significant as 2.9 and 1.8 million people, respectively, were forced to flee their countries to become refugees (United Nations High Commissioner for Refugees 2016a). A dramatic rise in the refugee population started in 2013, as shown in Figure 1.1. However, the

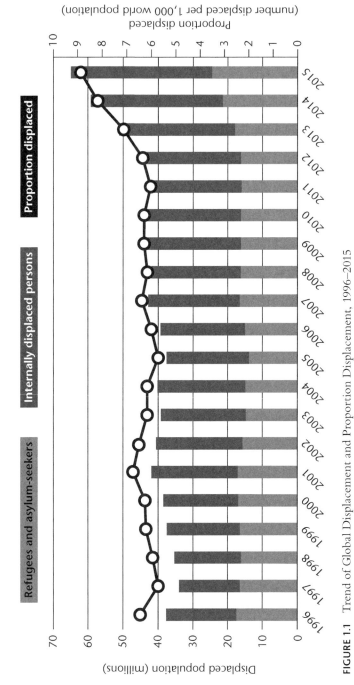

FIGURE 1.1 Trend of Global Displacement and Proportion Displacement, 1996–2015

Source: United Nations High Commissioner for Refugees (2016a:6)

rise in the last few years (with nine people per 1,000 being forcibly displaced, as opposed to six per 1,000 since 1999) has coincided with the Arab Spring and the prolonged Syrian conflict. Other unresolved conflicts such as those in Afghanistan, the Central African Republic, South Sudan, and Yemen, as well as some new or reignited conflicts, such as those in Burundi, Iraq, Libya, and Niger, have also contributed to the increase in these numbers.

The United Nations High Commissioner for Refugees (UNHCR) records that, by the end of 2015, global forced displacements (including "internally displaced persons") reached 65.3 million. This number includes forcibly displaced people that have fled "persecution, conflict, generalized violence, or human rights violations" (United Nations High Commissioner for Refugees 2016a: 2). Out of this number, 21.3 million are recognized as refugees (5.2 million of them are Palestinian refugees registered by the United Nations Relief and Works Agency for Palestine, UNRWA), 40.8 million are recognized as "internally displaced persons," and 3.2 million are recognized as "asylum seekers."

It is important to note that in 2015, developing regions hosted 86 percent of the world's refugees under the UNHCR's mandate, compared with about 70 percent two decades ago. The least developed countries have provided asylum to 4.2 million refugees, or about 26 percent of the global total, while at the same time struggling to meet the development needs of their own citizens. By far, the main receiving country is Turkey, with over 2.5 million refugees. Next on the list are Pakistan, Lebanon, and the Islamic Republic of Iran, as shown in Figure 1.2. Developed countries do not even appear on the list of the top 10 receiving countries. Lebanon is the first state on a list of countries that have a significant refugee-to-national population ratio, with nearly one in five residents being a refugee. When the number of refugees is recorded against the host country's gross domestic product measured in U.S. dollars, the Democratic Republic of the Congo has received 471 refugees per U.S. dollar of GDP, which confirms the strain of hosting refugees on that country. Ethiopia and Pakistan are also in a similar position (UNHCR 2016a:17).

Similar trends can be observed in regards to countries of origin: in 2015, the top ten countries of origin of refugees were located in the developing regions of the world. These ten source countries (presented in Figure 1.3) accounted for 76 percent of the global refugee population under the UNHCR's mandate. The Syrian Arab Republic was in 2015 (as it was in 2014) the top source country of refugees, with 4.9 million of its people residing elsewhere. The overwhelming majority of these refugees moved to one of the neighboring countries, mostly to Turkey, while major host countries outside the immediate region included Germany, Sweden, and Italy.

When the data regarding source and host countries are compared, it is confirmed that around 90 percent of the refugees find asylum in neighboring countries (Figure 1.4). It is apparent that host countries usually host refugees from one source

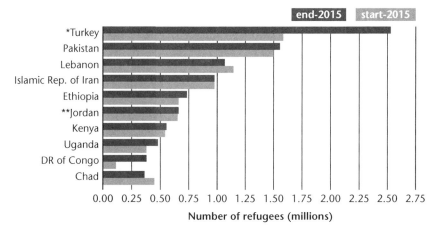

FIGURE 1.2 Major Refugee-Hosting Countries at the Start and End of 2015
Source: United Nations High Commissioner for Refugees (2016a: 15)

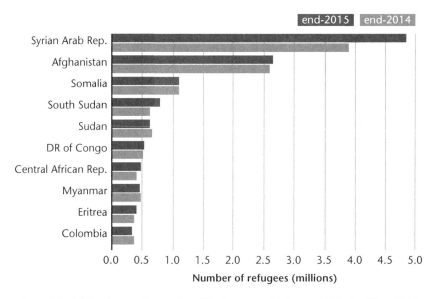

FIGURE 1.3 Major Source Countries of Refugees at the Start and End of Year 2015
Source: United Nations High Commissioner for Refugees (2016a: 16)

country; only Ethiopia has a somewhat equal number of people arriving from two countries—Somalia and South Sudan. Since these host countries are classified as "developing," with some of them as "least developed," it is unlikely that economic motives were the most important for these kinds of migrations. Moreover, since refugees have scarce resources available for their displacement,

FIGURE 1.4 The Flow of Refugees to Other Countries

Source: United Nations High Commissioner for Refugees (2016a:21)

it is challenging for most of them to embark on a longer journey; instead, they usually settle in the nearest safe area.

Europe's Migrant Crisis 2015

Although the number of refugees in all countries of the world peaked in 2014, only in the second half of 2015 did Europe witness a large influx. Hundreds of thousands of people embarked on a dangerous journey every month, most of them crossing the Mediterranean Sea to reach the shores of the European countries, with most of the refugees coming from the Syrian Arab Republic, Afghanistan, and Iraq. After entering the EU in Greece, most of them followed the Western Balkans route (as shown in Figure 1.5), leaving the EU to re-enter it in Hungary or Croatia before proceeding to other EU countries.

This situation resulted in over one million recorded migrant arrivals by sea in the countries of the European Union in 2015, compared to more than 200,000 arrivals by sea recorded in the previous year—five times the increase. The most commonly used route was from Turkey to the neighboring Greek islands in the Eastern Aegean Sea, an effective way to enter the EU until an agreement was reached between the EU and Turkey in March 2016. The deal stipulated that all migrants who did not apply for asylum in Greece would be sent back to Turkey; the same was to happen if their claim was rejected. While the UNHCR and other aid agencies criticized the agreement, equating it to mass expulsion that contravened international law and basic humanitarian principles, the deal nevertheless produced a rapid decrease in the number of migrants reaching the EU, with Italy re-claiming first place as a first-contact country for Mediterranean migrants, especially from African countries, but also from other migrants who found this route more acceptable now, as shown in the various UNHCR data.

Despite the stereotypes often portrayed in the media, relatively few refugees find their way to Western Europe: in 2015, there were 1.8 million detections of illegal border crossing along the EU's external borders and 1.26 million first-time asylum applicants in the EU, both relatively small numbers when one takes into account that globally 65.3 million people were forcibly displaced. Given the EU's estimated population of 510 million in January 2016, first-time asylum seekers account for less than 0.25 percent of the EU's population. Indeed, Sweden and Malta are the only European high-income countries present on the UNHCR's 2015 top ten list of states with a significant refugee-to-national population ratio. Each has 17 recorded refugees per 1,000 members of the national population (United Nations High Commissioner for Refugees 2016a:18).

The title of this chapter purposefully uses the word "migrant," rather than "refugee," because not everyone who seeks asylum is from an area that has recorded threats to individual existence. While refugees from countries such as Syria, Afghanistan, and Iraq have their asylum applications mostly approved in the EU, others are rejected and sent back to the point where they entered the

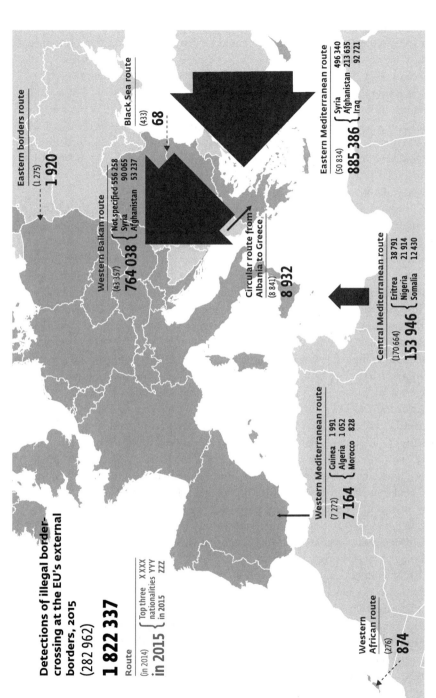

FIGURE 1.5 Dominant Migrant Routes and Number of Illegal Border Crossings

Source: FRONTEX (2016:16)

EU. Around 33 percent of people who illegally entered the EU in 2015 did not have specified nationalities or falsely claimed to have arrived from Syria (Frontex 2016) with no documented evidence of systematic threats or any evidence that they did in fact escape from immediate danger. Moreover, it was not uncommon for local migrants in the EU's neighborhood—people from Kosovo, Serbia, and Albania—to join the migration, seeking illegal ways to enter the EU and apply for asylum. Other economic migrants (for example, those from Nigeria, Gambia, and Pakistan) also joined this route. The question nevertheless remains: Why do refugees who come from life-threatening conflicts choose to travel to Western Europe, taking a journey that is life-threatening itself and which has an average price tag of several hundred U.S. dollars?

A recent study of asylum seekers traveling through the Western Balkans has revealed that most of them are "unmarried males at peak working age, from countries affected by war and political turmoil" (Lukić 2016). This suggests that we cannot easily divide migrants into groups of "economic" and "survival" migrants, as many of them who travel to the EU are a combination of both. Indeed, both of these variables are actually on a continuum of different conditions that are present in different countries and regions, and each migrant has his or her position on this continuum, each with his or her own unique story to share. Different individuals have different fears: many have faced forced military service, political persecution, religious oppression, ethnic violence, civil war, human trafficking, and organ harvesting. Other individuals seek to escape devastating poverty and hunger, while still others believe they could simply do better elsewhere.

An intriguing question in this situation is why did the number of migrants reaching EU's borders peak in 2015, when 2014 saw record numbers of refugees globally? One possible explanation is that refugees tend to follow routes that are more "beaten": The more people use one route, the more it becomes popular to others. Therefore, refugees could have been "pulled" toward the EU by people who fled there before them, illustrating to them that it is possible to enter illegally in the EU and settle there, given the high ratio of asylum acceptances, especially for Syrians. Some of these individuals had personal contacts in Western Europe with migrants who had already made the journey; others had been encouraged by what they had heard from others. The more that people fled to the EU, the more compelling the option appeared to others.

As more migrants sought to reach the EU, people smuggling operations became more developed, making it easier for anyone with enough money to decide to invest in a personal future in the EU. Refugees and smugglers are often in a symbiotic relationship (Salt 2000), and it is in their common interest to get the job done. No one in this chain wants to report a crime because of the significant benefits to both sides. Indeed, Europe has had problems with regulating human trafficking and people smuggling for decades; a UNHCR report from 2000 states that "the current status quo is practically and ethically bankrupt from all positions," (Morrison and Crosland 2000) with the EU, in practice, motivating migrants to enter illegally due to its strict asylum policies. As a result, this was the perfect place for smugglers to begin forming smuggling networks. Over 90 percent of migrants who enter the EU are aided in some way by members of criminal networks (UNHCR 2016b). The main corridors for migrants are usually well organized but also fluid and flexible. They adapt quickly to external factors, such as border controls, new border obstacles, and weather conditions. These are multinational businesses with agents around the globe, usually led by leaders who coordinate activities along any given route, and with organizers and facilitators at the local level. It is estimated that in 2015, people smuggling around the globe resulted in payments of 5 to 6 billion U.S. dollars (UNHCR 2016b). Most of the migrants pay for transport services in cash before they embark (52 percent), but alternative banking systems (such as hawala—an informal value transfer system based on the performance and honor of a huge network of money brokers) and payments from relatives already living in the EU also make a significant contribution (20 and 16 percent, respectively) (UNHCR 2016b). Moreover, the smuggling business extends further on both sides: Smugglers need to launder their money and thus may engage local economies; people who are smuggled sometimes engage in criminal activities to pay for their travel or are victims of labor or sexual exploitation. Further, the terrorist attacks in Paris in 2015 also showed that terrorists can use these networks to infiltrate the EU.

This combination of large numbers of people who had already migrated to the EU and well-organized transportation networks created a significant "pull" factor, one paralleling the existing economic "pull" factor of the target countries. This influx also coincided with the amendments made to the asylum law of the Former Yugoslav Republic of Macedonia in 2015, which allowed for a 72-hour period of legal transit and access to public transportation for all refugees and other asylum seekers. Similarly, for several months the Serbian government arranged public transport for, as well as the rapid processing of, migrants.

The declaration made in Germany in late August 2015 that there was "no upper limit to the right for asylum" also encouraged various refugees and economic migrants to try their luck by applying for asylum. These factors probably strengthened the perception that an illegal journey to the EU was easy, fast, and successful, which likely contributed to the decisions of refugees in Turkey to move westwards. Additionally, when public pressure forced European countries to start reassessing their asylum practices, an additional "pull" factor was created: many refugees decided to act quickly in an attempt to enter the EU as soon as possible and before the doors closed. This resulted in large numbers of asylum-seeking migrants in the last days of the prevailing status quo. After countries in Central Europe closed their borders and tightened border controls, many migrants were "locked" in transit countries, such as Serbia and the Former Yugoslav Republic of Macedonia. Some even had to temporarily settle in a "no man's land" between national borders. As a result, this route was largely abandoned by most migrants in 2016.

Conclusion

The facts in the previous sections were presented with the aim of explaining various aspects of the European migrant crisis in 2015. While this was not the first-time that a refugee crisis challenged the political, ethical, and humanitarian conditions of another region, multiple "push" and "pull" factors coincided in this crisis, creating a tsunami of migrants that flooded the European institutions designed to process and accommodate refugees. Simply put, hundreds of thousands of refugees and/or economic migrants found that the EU had its doors open, and decided to pass through those doors.

It was also argued that it is not easy (or acceptable in most cases) to classify somebody as a "refugee" as opposed to an "economic migrant." Many asylum seekers in the EU have complex pasts and contexts, and in order to manage a crisis like this, we must understand the complexity of motives that impel people to embark on such a dangerous journey, burdened with their past and tempted to illegally cross international borders.

The future challenges are two-fold: how to manage the existing migrants and how to manage future migrant crises. These challenges generate different questions: What did the EU learn from this experience? Is asylum seeking becoming obsolete in the ever-changing environment and in a globally connected world? How do we tackle large groups of people who believe they deserve better? How do we decide what is enough and when it is enough when dealing with migration? And is there enough at all?

References

Davenport, Christian A., Will H. Moore, and Steven C. Poe. 2003. "Sometimes You Just Have to Leave: Domestic Threats and Forced Migration, 1964–1989." *International Interactions* 29(1):27–55.

Frontex. 2016. "Risk Analysis for 2016." Report number 2499/2016. Warsaw: Frontex.

Hansen, Randall and Desmond King. 2000. "Illiberalism and the New Politics of Asylum: Liberalism's Dark Side." *Political Quarterly* 71(4):396–403.

Lukić, Vesna. 2016. "Understanding Transit Asylum Migration: Evidence from Serbia." *International Migration* 54(4):31–44.

Moore, Will H. and Stephen M. Shellman. 2004. "Fear of Persecution: Forced Migration, 1952–1995." *Journal of Conflict Resolution* 40(5):723–45.

Morrison, Andrew R. 1993. "Violence or Economics: What Drives Internal Migration in Guatemala?" *Economic Development and Cultural Change* 41(4):817–31.

Morrison, John and Beth Crosland. 2000. "The Trafficking and Smuggling of Refugees: The End Game in European Asylum Policy?" UNHCR.

Neumayer, Eric. 2005. "Bogus Refugees? The Determinants of Asylum Migration to Western Europe." *International Studies Quarterly* 49(3):389–410.

Salt, John. 2000. "Trafficking and Human Smuggling: A European Perspective." *International Migration* 38(3):31–56.

Schmeidl, Susanne. 1997. "Exploring the Causes of Forced Migration: A Pooled Time-Series Analysis, 1971–1990." *Social Science Quarterly* 78(2):284–308.

Stanley, William D. 1987. "Economic Migrants or Refugees from Violence? A Time-Series Analysis of Salvadoran Migration to the United States." *Latin American Research Review* 22(1):132–54.

United Nations High Commissioner for Refugees. 2016a. "Global Trends: Forced Displacement in 2015." Geneva: UNHCR. Retrieved March 1, 2017 (www.unhcr.org/576408cd7.pdf).

United Nations High Commissioner for Refugees. 2016b. "Migrant Smuggling Networks: Joint Europol-Interpol Report Executive Summary." *Europol and Interpol*. Retrieved March 1, 2017 (www.europol.europa.eu/sites/default/files/documents/ep-ip_report_executive_summary.pdf).

2

SERBIA AND THE MIGRATION CRISIS

The Power of Framing

Karthika Sasikumar

SAN JOSE STATE UNIVERSITY

Political and Military Sociology: An Annual Review, 2017, Vol. 45: 18–35.

This chapter examines Serbian policy towards refugees or migrants from 2015 to mid-2016. It finds that the Serbian government framed the population movement as "transit through Serbia." This choice allowed it to benefit from favorable reporting in the international media, and forced European Union leaders to engage Serbia in resolving the crisis. At the same time, the government was able to avoid the costs associated with the integration of refugees. The transit frame also had unintended consequences: creating uncertainty about legal status, fostering opportunities for smugglers and exploitation, impeding a comprehensive and durable solution to refugee flows, and de-legitimizing the state in the long term. Most studies of migration have focused on the humanitarian, social, and economic consequences of population movements. This article calls on political scientists to contribute to the conversation, by analyzing the frame in which migration is presented to domestic and international audiences. Paying attention to framing would also help policy-makers to identify lacunae in a country's response as a result of framing.

Introduction

As a consequence of the violent and protracted civil war in Syria, many Syrians were forced to seek refuge in Europe. A large influx of Syrian refugees was soon mixed with an even larger population of people from other countries beset by strife and economic maladies, such as Afghanistan, Eritrea, Iraq, and Pakistan.

Serbia, along with other European countries, struggled to deal with this influx of migrants. This article examines Serbia's policy towards refugees or migrants in 2015 and 2016. It finds that the Serbian government framed the population movement as "transit through Serbia." This article examines the reasons behind the choice of this "transit" frame. It describes the positive and negative consequences—both intended and unintended—of this choice. After providing a brief historical background in the first section, the article introduces the concept of framing. The second section elaborates on the claim that the "transit" frame was dominant in the government's presentation of the refugee crisis inside Serbia, as well as to foreign audiences. In the third section, the article explains the reasons why this frame was chosen. The transit frame had consequences, some of which were unexpected. The article analyzes these major consequences—both positive and negative—in the fourth section. In the concluding section, the article draws out implications for theory and policy.

Background: Serbia as Origin, Host, and Transit Country

When it comes to migration, Serbia is at the same time a country of origin, a transit country, and a host country. Government sources estimate the size of the worldwide Serbian diaspora at 3.5 million (Ministry of Foreign Affairs n.d.). Even if this is not an accurate figure, it is undeniable that Serbia has been for centuries a source of out-migration to countries in Europe and other parts of the world—notably Australia, Canada, and the United States.

In the 1980s, there was a steady stream of migrants leaving the Socialist Federal Republic of Yugoslavia (SFRY), of which Serbia was the biggest unit. A huge spike in out-migration from Serbia was the consequence of the internecine wars of the 1990s. These wars ended in the breakup of the SFRY and the formation of the independent nations of Bosnia-Herzegovina, Croatia, the Former Yugoslav Republic of Macedonia, Montenegro, Serbia, and Slovenia. Kosovo declared independence in 2008; however, Serbia does not recognize the declaration and considers Kosovo to be an autonomous province within its territory. In Serbia, which attempted and failed to resist the dissolution of the SFRY, the wars took a heavy toll. The cessation of hostilities was followed by a period of sluggish economic growth characterized by high youth unemployment; those who were able to build their lives in more prosperous countries left Serbia. It is estimated that around 300,000 educated young people have exited Serbia in the past 25 years (Jukić 2013). In the 2000–2010 period, as a result of war and displacement, Serbia was among the world's top five countries in the number of applications for asylum in European countries. In the five-year period prior to that, it was the top country with respect to the number of asylum seekers in European countries (Vujadinović et al. 2013:55–7).

It is important to note that Kosovo, which as per Serbian law is a constituent province, is a major source of refugee flows to Europe. In the first three months of 2015, more than 50,000 Kosovars sought asylum in the European Union. However, by May of that year, asylum applications from Syrians alone equaled those from all of the Western Balkans (Freedom House 2016). Consequently, Serbia's position as a *country of origin* of refugees became less significant.

Serbia has also received migrants as a *host country*. In 2010 Serbia was home to the largest number of forced migrants in Europe (Nikitović and Lukić 2010). During the breakup of Yugoslavia in the early 1990s along ethnic lines, people who found themselves on the wrong side of the ethnic divide were forced to leave their homes and move to regions where their co-ethnics were in the majority. The government of Serbia made special arrangements to accommodate those of Serbian origin who had been forced to emigrate from Bosnia and Croatia (and, in the 2000s, from Kosovo). Although at different periods of time the Serbian government claimed the territories from which they migrated as part of Serbia, those fleeing were referred to as "refugees" both in common and government discourse and were treated as such. The Commissariat for Refugees was established in 1992. Acknowledging Serbia's position as a source, transit, and host country for migrants, this institution was renamed the Commissariat for Refugees and Migration in 2012.

Serbia's geographical location on the edges of the European Union contributes to its role as a *transit country*—one that temporarily hosts migrants as they pass through solely in order to reach their final destination. As a transit country, Serbia faces certain challenges. For example, concerns about the trafficking of children and women through Serbia led to the designation of Serbia as a Tier 2 country in the U.S. State Department's annual reports on human trafficking (U.S. Department of State 2016).[1] Aware of the negative reputational consequences of Serbia's association with trafficking (Fosson 2011: 184–5), the government in Belgrade adopted its first National Strategy on Combating Human Trafficking in 2006 and, since then, has changed its legal framework several times with the goal of halting human trafficking.

The influx of refugees that is the subject of this volume began in 2015 and peaked in the latter half of that year. It is important to clarify some terminology at the outset. The term "refugee" has a specific meaning in international law. Therefore, people who are not specifically fleeing war or internal violence are more properly termed "migrants." In reality, however, it is difficult and almost impossible to maintain this distinction. Many people fleeing a war zone are not menaced directly by the violence, but see no way to make a livelihood—yet they are not simply economic migrants. Similarly, countries with shattered economies may also be experiencing high levels of armed violence, though they are not technically at war.

These realities have led international organizations to come up with terms such as "*prima facie* refugees" or "persons likely in need of international protection."[2] Since the granting of international refugee status is a complicated and protracted process, international organizations have agreed to treat vulnerable populations as equivalent to refugees. This helps them to quickly respond to humanitarian needs, while avoiding the legal implications of refugee status.

This article does not take a position on the legal status of the population movements and deals only with the manner in which the population movements are handled by governments. Thus, it uses the terms "refugee" and "migrant" interchangeably. Moreover, the article does not purport to evaluate the efficacy of the Serbian state's response to the population movement that it faces. Such an evaluation would require deep knowledge of the situation through field work on location. Instead, the article focuses on the rhetorical presentation of the issue by Serbian leaders, aiming to show that the framing of the issue has important effects on ground realities.

Accurate data on the numbers of migrants are hard to come by. The United Nations High Commissioner for Refugees (UNHCR) estimates that 66,000 people entered Serbia in the first half of 2015 (Lukić 2016:33). In the first six months of 2016, an estimated 100,000 refugees transited through Serbia (Pantović 2016). Initially, the most popular route for migrants was passage through Serbia, first to Hungary, and later towards Croatia and Slovenia. The migrants entered Serbia either from Greece through the Former Yugoslav Republic of Macedonia or from Bulgaria, if originating in Turkey. This was termed "the Balkan route" to Europe.

An agreement between the European Union and Turkey in March 2016 led to the closure of borders across the region, leaving migrants trapped in Serbia and the Former Yugoslav Republic of Macedonia. In the autumn of 2016, an estimated 5000 refugees and migrants remained in Serbia, out of which approximately 46 percent were men, 16 percent were women, and 38 percent were children. The majority of refugees come from Afghanistan (44 percent), Syria (21 percent), and Iraq (9 percent) (International Organization for Migration 2016).

The reception of refugees in Serbia has been, overall, positive. This is especially true in contrast with their treatment at the hands of neighboring countries such as Bulgaria and Hungary (Anon 2016a, 2016b; Damjanović 2016; Denti 2015; Djokić 2015). One article, with the provocative title, "Wait, the Serbs are now the good guys?," claimed that a mere 15 years previously, Serbia was "an international pariah, shunned for its role in the Yugoslav wars, and perceived as the instigator of ethnic conflict and persecution. Now government and civil society have won praise for the compassion with which the current crisis has been handled" (Macdowall 2015). Indeed, Serbia saw no significant protests organized against migrants and asylum seekers (Damjanović 2016:6).

Framing the Migrant Issue in Serbia

Erving Goffman used the concept of framing to describe how an individual constructs reality. He wrote that social frameworks provide "background understanding for events" and guide active human agents in their deeds (Goffman 1986: 22). In political science, the idea that metaphorical framing can shape political outcomes was popularized by the linguist George Lakoff (Lakoff 2009). One important question remains: since metaphorical framing occurs at the individual level, how can it explain the collective meanings that are *shared* by elites and mass publics and which drive decision-making? Constructivist scholar William Flanik suggests an answer to this question. He recommends that we think of metaphorical frames as constitutive of ideational structure and framing as a socio-cognitive practice that produces (and changes) structure (Flanik 2011:431).

The concept of framing in political science is most popular among scholars of social movements and in studies of political communication. Scholars of social movements have enlarged the concept of framing to refer to how contention is framed by actors (including the state itself), their opponents, third parties, and the media. Frames must draw on existing dominant values but also move beyond them (Tarrow 2011: 144–5). To be successful, frames must be resonant with pre-existing, culturally familiar concepts. A successful frame needs a high degree of strategic modularity, which means that terms that emerge in one strategic context can be transferred to others without losing the strategic advantages they originally possessed (Tarrow 2013: 193–4). Robert Entman, who studies political communication, identifies two aspects of framing: substantive and procedural. Substantive frames perform four functions: they define conditions or effects as problematic, identify causes, convey moral judgment, and propose remedy. Procedural frames evaluate which actors are legitimate (Entman 2004: 5–6).

The dominant frame that the Serbian government has adopted to represent and explain the refugee influx is that of "transit." The observable implications of this framing include:

- openness towards the entry of refugees into the territory of Serbia
- reluctance to integrate refugees into permanent social structures such as educational institutions or the job market
- readiness to defend refugees from direct attacks and to cater to their urgent needs
- refusal to take responsibility for their ultimate fate and invocation of external (European) responsibility

This article argues that, since we observe all four of these in the treatment of refugees in Serbia in 2015 and 2016, the "transit country" frame was dominant. Like most issues in the sphere of external relations, the government took the lead in determining the framing, which was then picked up and deployed by the news media. While non-governmental organizations dealing with refugees on the ground saw the flaws in the framing, they did not overtly resist it. Even international organizations, which had to cooperate with the Serbian government, adopted the framing to a great extent.

The Choice of the Transit Country Frame

Although the facts of the case favor the choice of the "transit country" frame, the choice was not inevitable. There are five main reasons why the Serbian government chose to frame the migrant movement as transit through the territory of Serbia. These are:

- objective reality
- lack of material resources
- sensitivity to public opinion
- concern about international reputation
- imperatives of integration into the European Union

The most important reason for the transit frame is that the overwhelming majority of migrants did not originally intend to stay in Serbia. Thus, the frame corresponds with objective reality. It must be noted, however, that the reality itself is changing. Initially, migrants intended to only transit through Serbia. However, as the countries that were their preferred destinations began to erect barriers to their entry, these migrants found themselves unable to transit. They were forced to spend much longer than planned in Serbia and could be residing there for the foreseeable future.

The second reason for the framing of Serbia as a transit country has to do with the material resources available to the Serbian state. Serbia can be characterized as a middle-income country. In comparison to EU member states, Serbia ranks at the very bottom of the list. Serbia's gross domestic product (GDP) was 35 percent of the EU average in 2012, and the average purchasing power of residents was 43 percent of the EU average (Miletić 2013). Following the global economic crisis in 2008, Serbia's economy experienced a downturn and state budgets were under pressure. The transit framing enabled the government to avoid the larger expenditures associated with permanently housing and caring for refugees.

The third reason for the framing is rooted in domestic politics. On the one hand, the government headed by Prime Minister Aleksandar Vučić benefited from a relatively stable polity. Vučić's party, the Serbian Progressive Party, won the elections in the spring of 2016 with just below 50 percent of the vote and formed a government with coalition partners. Public opinion continued to be supportive, as seen in a poll from July 2016 in which the ruling party commanded the support of 47.5 percent of the respondents (Nova Srpska Politička Misao 2016). On the other hand, the political mood in Serbia has been quite volatile, with intense contestation among parties. Thus, the government might be reluctant to embrace the refugee inflow.

This is especially true if there are reasons to think that public opinion would be *hostile* to refugees. We note that, in this region, religious identity and definitions of belonging have caused major wars in the recent past. First, Serbia today is characterized by high ethnic homogeneity, and most citizens have little direct experience with multicultural co-existence and tolerance of religious and ethnic minorities. This is especially true of the youngest generation of citizens—those who were born after 1990 and who came of age in a Serbia that was designed to be the homeland of Orthodox Serbs. As per the last census, close to 85 percent of the population is Serb (and Orthodox), with people of Hungarian (3.5 percent), Bosnian (2 percent), and Croatian (.8 percent) origin having small minority populations. The Roma people are the only visible/racial minority (2 percent). These figures do not include the population living in Kosovo (Statistical Office of the Republic of Serbia 2012). Second, right-wing groups and political parties seized on the refugee crisis to confront the government, accusing the leaders in Belgrade of kowtowing to European countries and allowing the entry of migrants who could pose a security threat (Dveri 2016).

At the same time, it has been suggested that the country's past experience with war and migrant streams has made it *more tolerant* of refugees and that Serbs are more empathetic towards refugees because they have been refugees themselves or hosted refugees (Denti 2015; Djinović and Popović 2015; Macdowall 2015; Pupavac and Pupavac 2015; Subasić 2015). This narrative draws on Serbia's identity as a *host* country for refugees. Serbian elites also reminded the public that Serbia was a *source* country for refugees since many Serbian citizens fled to Western Europe during the breakup of Yugoslavia in the 1990s (Damjanović 2016:5).

On an institutional level, the prior experience of dealing with refugees from the breakup of Yugoslavia helped with capacity-building in government institutions and civil society. Those responsible for tackling the crisis point out that, unlike neighboring countries, Serbia had mechanisms in place for dealing with large population movements.[3]

It must be noted that there are major differences between the co-ethnic refugees from the 1990s wars and those in the current wave. It is estimated that 90 percent of the co-ethnic refugees were accommodated in private homes (Weiss and Pasić 1997:45). This indicates that the co-ethnic refugees were part of social networks that would shelter and provide for them. As one official put it, the co-ethnic refugees were "easier to receive." The Commissariat, which was set up with the goal of integrating refugees into Serbian society, found itself in 2015 facing migrants who had no intention of putting down roots in Serbia.[4]

As Ana Bracic points out, on the one hand we may expect that previous experience of violence and displacement would lead to altruistic behavior towards newly arrived refugees. On the other hand, considering that most of the refugees are foreigners and, therefore, members of an out-group, altruistic behavior might not extend to them (Bracic 2016). We also note that anti-Muslim sentiment persists in Serbia after the experience of wars in Bosnia and Kosovo (Pavlović 2016:63). Thus, displaced Serbs may be particularly unsympathetic to the newly arriving refugees who are mostly Muslim or are usually perceived to be Muslim

(Bracic 2016). In fact, the high number of co-ethnic refugees that entered Serbia in the past may have actually made it a *tougher* host country for refugees that are not co-ethnics. Marta Stojić-Mitrović notes that in the current discourse, "refugee" is equated with "national" or "co-ethnic refugee." Consequently, foreigners tend to be perceived as migrants impelled by economic motives, rather than as refugees (Stojić-Mitrović 2014:1118).

Public opinion data are unhelpful in capturing the public's response to refugees. There are few rigorous studies of tolerance in the population, and the evidence is mixed. Over 35 percent of the respondents in a survey conducted in 2013 had negative views of minority religious communities (Centar za Slobodne Izbore i Demokratiju 2013:14). Yet another survey found that respondents in Serbia were generally *more favorably disposed* towards minorities and refugees than those in neighboring countries (Regional Cooperation Council 2016:43). In a public opinion poll of 1000 respondents in May 2015 (which was heavily biased towards unemployed, housewives, and retired persons), almost three-quarters of respondents (73.2 percent) stated that the key reasons for asylum seekers leaving their home country were war, insecurity, and fear of persecution. Only one out of ten respondents believed that the main reason was to improve their standard of living (Ninamedia 2015).

Considering that there is no obvious constituency supportive of the refugees, it is no wonder that the government in Belgrade was reluctant to expend political capital and focused, instead, on providing humanitarian care. Thus, as has been noticed, the "Serbian government has built the national consensus on refugees on the presumption that refugees won't stay" (Pupavac and Pupavac 2015).

The fourth reason for the transit frame is that it allowed Serbia to make a good impression on external audiences (Pavlović 2016; Pupavac and Pupavac 2015). Serbian leaders realized that their handling of the situation would be closely watched around the world. Donatella Bradić of the International Organization for Migration (IOM) agrees that the Vučić government "saw the opportunity to play the good guy for once."[5] This was particularly important since the country has acquired negative associations—ethnic cleansing, intolerance, poverty, and so on. These negative associations are quantified in a recent study which lists Serbia's low position in various indices, such as the East West Nation Brand Perception Index, the Global Competitiveness Index, and the Travel and Tourism Competitiveness index (Nikolić and Bodroža 2012). In her view, the refugee crisis was actually a win-win situation for Serbia—one in which the *right* thing to do was also the *smart* thing to do. By meeting the urgent, short-term needs of the refugees, the Serbian government was able to improve its international image.

In addition, Serbia's international reputation was also linked to its legal obligations to refugees and asylum seekers under the international treaties and agreements it has signed. Serbia is a signatory to the 1951 United Nations Convention on Refugees and its 1967 Protocol (generally referred to as the Geneva Convention). Article 57 of Serbia's Constitution guarantees the right to asylum, which is elaborated in legislation such as the Law on Asylum, the Law on Foreigners, the Law on Migration Management, the General Administrative Procedure Act, and the Administrative Disputes Act. In 2013, the Ministry of Interior started drafting a new asylum law. The Asylum Office is in charge of applying the asylum procedure, while the Commissariat for Refugees and Migration assumes responsibility for the accommodation and integration of people granted asylum or subsidiary protection (Lilyanova 2016:3). In line with advanced democracies, Serbia guarantees, to both asylum seekers and those already granted asylum, rights to residence, basic living conditions, health care, education, social assistance, and labor market access.

In addition to being concerned about their country's international reputation, the government in Belgrade was also (probably more) concerned about Serbia's reputation among European countries. The integration of Serbia into Europe, as exemplified by accession to the EU, is currently the top foreign policy priority of the Vučić government. This is also its most controversial strategy since support for EU accession is volatile and has been on a downward trend. A survey conducted in Serbia in the last weeks of 2015 found that less than half of the respondents wanted their country to become a member of the European Union. Interestingly, in the same survey, 49 percent of the respondents feared that migrants from the Middle East/North Africa posed a "very big threat" to the stability of Europe (Center for Insights in Survey Research 2016).

Serbia's position as an aspiring EU member made the "transit" frame more attractive for two reasons. First, Serbia has been a candidate for EU membership since 2012. The accession process involves lengthy periodic negotiations, which are often influenced by current events. In July 2016, Serbia and the EU started negotiations on Chapter 24, dealing with the area designated as "Justice, Freedom, and Security," which incorporates asylum and migration policies. If EU officials judge that Serbia is not in harmony with the EU in this area, it could lead to a complete suspension of negotiations (Lilyanova 2016:6). By framing the refugees as merely transiting through Serbia, the country was able to avoid tough questions about its policies on migration and asylum.

Second, an efficient border security service is considered a crucial requirement for EU candidacy (Collantes-Celador and Juncos 2012:203). Accordingly, the Serbian government explicitly states that integration into EU migration management and control systems is one of its goals (Stojić-Mitrović 2014). Serbia is conscious of the need to shield EU members from an influx of refugees. It was therefore important not to be perceived as a country housing refugees who were battering at the door of Europe.

At the same time that Serbia was expected to manage migration flows, it was expected to do so in accordance with European values. As Neovi M. Karakatsanis argues elsewhere in this volume, openness to migrants, the fair and humane treatment of asylum seekers, and living up to one's international obligations toward non-nationals are presented as quintessentially European values. Belgrade lost no time in linking Serbian policy to these values. "We treated refugees far better than some EU countries: we didn't use tear gas and no one attacked them," commented Prime Minister Vučić. "We speak about desperate people, not about criminals or terrorists," he continued, confirming that Serbia would never erect walls or fences against them. Indeed, Serbia even pledged to accept a number of Syrian refugees as part of the EU-wide reallocation mechanism, as if it were an EU member state. "We are more European than some Europeans when it comes to migrants and some other issues," he emphasized (Denti 2015). Moreover, following the use of water cannon, pepper spray, and tear gas on migrants by Hungarian police, Vučić was swift to condemn Budapest's behavior as "non-European" (Macdowall 2015). Filip Kovačević's contribution to this volume elaborates on this strategy, which he characterizes as one of "raising the hypocrisy costs" to EU members.

While Serbia invoked European values, it has been pointed out that wealthy European nations have failed to live up to these values in their reception of migrants (Greenhill 2016). As Danijela Dudley's essay in this volume notes, the EU response was inconsistent. The ripple effect of this inconsistency affects even non-EU members such as Albania, the Former Yugoslav Republic of Macedonia, and Serbia. As Donatella Bradić points out, governments in Belgrade and other European capitals will try to align with EU policy. If there is no EU policy, national interests will become dominant.[6]

Because the Serbian government wanted Brussels to recognize the vital position of Serbia in the migration crisis, it chose a frame where the EU appears as the final destination and Serbia as a country of transit. Serbia was able to "display European values at little or no cost" (Pavlović 2016:60). The Minister for Labor, Aleksandar Vulin, demanded that Serbia must be equal to EU member states in terms of monetary, technical, and other aid programs (Anon 2016c). The EU supported Serbian efforts to the tune of €40 million in the year starting September 2015 (European Union delegation to Serbia 2016). Since Serbia is not yet a member of the EU, there were obstacles in the way of effective coordination and communication. Consequently, Vulin was compelled to explicitly demand that Serbia should be part of a political solution to the migration crisis (Anon 2015).

As the Serbian government watched neighboring countries locking out migrants, it became concerned that the refugees would be stuck in Serbia. Yet it refused to contemplate the possibility of permanently integrating the migrants and continued to adhere to the "transit" frame (Anon 2015). The Prime Minister put it plainly when he said, "Serbia cannot be Europe's first and last defence" (InSerbia 2016). His Foreign Minister warned the EU not to treat Serbia as a "collection center" (Macdowall 2015). An official from the Commissariat mentioned that "Europe lacks a unified answer to the problem." He explained that Serbia is not a cause of the flight of people out of Syria, nor is it their final destination, but it is on their way. Once the Balkan route was no longer functioning, however, Serbian authorities found themselves in charge of people who were (and are) frustrated because they only want to be on their way and are unwilling to stay.[7]

Consequences of the "Transit" Frame

The previous section has listed the reasons why the transit frame became the obvious choice for the government in Belgrade. The argument does not assume that all authorities sincerely believed that this was the only possible presentation of the situation. Whether it was the most appropriate formulation or not, the transit frame had certain positive and negative consequences. This section addresses four such consequences:

- creating uncertainty about legal status
- fostering opportunities for smugglers and exploitation
- impeding a comprehensive and durable solution to refugee flows
- creating potential mistrust of the state in the long-term

As explained earlier, refugee status is granted after a lengthy legal process. Serbia is unable to efficiently process applications for refugee status. In 2014 only six refugee statuses and 12 subsidiary protections were granted. Moreover, Serbia declared the Former Yugoslav Republic of Macedonia, Turkey, and Greece to be "safe third countries," meaning that refugees could be compelled to return to those countries. Scholars conclude that the country lacks integration policies to facilitate the social inclusion of persons with recognized international protection (Kogovšek Šalamon 2016:5).

There is no legal framework for dealing with the vast majority of migrants who do not apply for asylum.[8] The temporary solution to the problem is the granting of a permit to remain in Serbia for 72 hours. The formal name of the permit is the Certificate of Expressed Intention to Seek Asylum and it is known informally as the "72 hour paper." Those without this certificate, or who have exceeded time limit, may be arrested for illegal entry and prosecuted. However, as the crisis progressed, the government became more relaxed in the implementation of its regulations on illegal entry. As per law, this is a misdemeanor that could lead to prosecution followed by a fine. However, the government is not trying hard to identify and prosecute illegal entrants because it relies on the refugees' motivation to leave Serbia. Finally, when apprehended, refugees have been advised by human rights organizations to declare that they are seeking asylum—which immediately confers legal rights on them.

Anyone coming into contact with the "illegals" is under obligation to report them to the police. Ordinary citizens are under a (mostly theoretical) obligation to conduct "document checks" and reproduce borders and divisions between legality and "illegality" everywhere, not just at the physical border. Any commercial transaction with an undocumented individual makes ordinary people—shopkeepers and boarding house owners—liable to prosecution for facilitating illegal border crossing and smuggling (Stojić-Mitrović and Meh 2016:630).

The creation of borders facilitates the business of those who want to breach them. Smuggling of goods and persons is a direct result of governments legislating border controls that they are not in a position to enforce. A clear example of this process in the Balkans was elaborated in the story of the siege of Sarajevo (Andreas 2008). During the siege, black marketers, smugglers, and other criminals prospered by running the blockade of the city by Bosnian Serb forces, which made it impossible for ordinary citizens to access essential goods and services. Similarly, trafficking of women in the Balkans is also facilitated by strict border controls and restrictions on movement that can only be overcome by criminals (Lindstrom 2007). In the case of refugees, the transit frame and the subsequent legal uncertainty lead to a precarious situation for migrants. Unlike in other countries, migrants were not forcibly herded or confined in camps; neither, however, were they properly processed and provided with legal aid. Instead, the main concern in Belgrade was to hasten them on their way with as little government involvement as possible. Thus, migrants who found themselves stuck in Serbia fell prey to people smugglers as it became progressively harder to cross borders while traveling on their own.[9]

Thus, by sticking to the "transit" frame, the current government of Serbia is adopting the policy of "kicking the can down the road," which is problematic for the long-term stability of the country. This article only examines a short time period of approximately two years in a rapidly changing scenario. However, we do know that 86 percent of the respondents in a 2015 survey by Ninamedia predicted that the migrants would not stay in Serbia (Ninamedia 2015). Yet, at the start of 2017, the UNHCR estimated that 6400 refugees were still living in Serbia (Marinković 2017).

As ordinary people become more affected by refugees, clashes become more likely. It is important to note that even co-ethnic refugees from Bosnia and Croatia were viewed negatively (and to some extent still are) by the local population. They were seen as a strain on the meager resources of the state at a time when the Serbian economy was in bad shape.[10] We can predict that migrants from South and West Asia will also increasingly be seen as problematic. It has been noted that residents of Belgrade have commented on the clothing, phones, and other possessions of the migrants, comparing them to their own and concluding that they are not "real refugees."[11]

Serbian society is used to viewing migration as a humanitarian issue.[12] This is supported by the finding in the 2015 Ninamedia poll that close to half of the respondents mentioned "pity" as the dominant emotion they felt towards refugees (Ninamedia 2015). In the longer term, however, migration will become intertwined with issues of resources and development, which will be a real test of the toleration of migrants. The reputational challenge for Serbia will grow as the number of migrants and the length of their stay increases.

The mainstream media's coverage of refugees has been remarkably positive. Since the government's control over the media is widely acknowledged, we can conclude that the debate has been framed in a positive way thanks to state intervention (Macdowall 2015). The government chose to suppress right-wing protest against migrants (for instance, by denying permits for protest marches) (Jovanović 2016). This was in service of framing the refugees as temporary problems and objects of pity.

At the same time, reports that refugees were responsible for some criminal activity (and that the government was covering it up) circulated in Belgrade's social networks. The danger is that when the situation changes for the worse and refugees become a semi-permanent presence, the public will lose trust in the government as well as in such civil society institutions as the media.

In November 2016, the government of Serbia issued an "Open Letter" to the "international humanitarian and non-government organizations which provide support and humanitarian assistance to the migrant population outside the permanent centers for asylum and transit reception centers." This letter, the legality of which is uncertain, informs the organizations that their work outside the government-run centers is "unacceptable" (Ivanisević 2016). The letter demonstrates that the government views such organizational efforts as undermining the state's control over migrants and that it wants to ban their efforts so that migrants are discouraged from entering or residing in Serbia. Thus, it appears that the state wants to remove the refugees from the view of ordinary citizens and render them invisible (Botić 2016). Finally, the letter is also a testimony to the absence of an integrated strategy and a state-civil society partnership, which are essential in tackling the migration issue.

The reluctance to seek a durable solution could also create problems in foreign relations. Serbia could be perceived as creating problems for its neighbors if it falls short in sheltering migrants or if it imposes requirements stringent enough to force migrants to leave for neighboring countries. This is particularly important in the context of European integration. As one official said, "The underlying dynamic with the accession process must be noted. Serbia is sensitive to pressure from Brussels to be, on the one hand, in accordance with the obligations under the 1951 Convention and, on the other hand, to be gatekeepers for Europe."[13] It is clear, then, that Europe is constraining Serbian freedom of action—and at times the constraints are at cross purposes. It is important to note that James Ker-Lindsay predicts a backlash against the EU as the refugee problem persists if, in the Serbian citizens' perception, the EU is dumping migrants on Serbia (Macdowall 2015).

Conclusion: Implications for Theory and Practice

The Serbian government, faced with a large population movement over which it had little control, chose to frame itself as a "country of transit." It was able to garner several political rewards with this choice: while avoiding the costs of integration of refugees, the government benefited from favorable reporting in the international press and forced European leaders to engage it in resolving the crisis. At the same time, the transit frame became harder to sustain as the countries surrounding Serbia started closing their borders, leaving refugees in Serbia. As this occurred, the negative consequences of the frame became more obvious. In particular, this frame made it less likely that there would be a long-term and concerted effort to solve the refugee crisis in conjunction with civil society institutions.

Most studies of migration have focused on the humanitarian, social, and economic consequences of population movements. This article calls on political scientists to contribute to the conversation by analyzing *the manner in which the problem is presented* to domestic and international audiences. As the article has shown, the framing of the issue has real consequences both for the receiving state, its neighbors, as well as for the well-being of the migrants themselves.

Paying greater attention to framing would also benefit policy-makers in the European bureaucracy and international humanitarian agencies. They would be able to identify lacunae in a country's response as a result of framing. In the case of Serbia described here, international actors should be concerned that public opinion is inadequately prepared for the long-term presence of refugees and that the government is unwilling to include NGOs as partners in dealing with the crisis.

Notes

1 Tier 2 countries are those that do not fully comply with the minimum standards of the U.S legislation, the Trafficking Victims Protection Act, but are making significant efforts to bring themselves into compliance with those standards.
2 Personal interview with Donatella Bradić and Marko Perović, International Organization for Migration, Belgrade, Serbia, October 3, 2016.
3 Personal interviews with Ivan Misković, Belgrade, Serbia, October 18, 2016; with Donatella Bradić, Belgrade, Serbia, October 3, 2016.
4 Personal interview with Ivan Misković, Belgrade, Serbia, October 18, 2016.
5 Personal interview with Donatella Bradić, Belgrade, Serbia, October 3, 2016.
6 Personal interview with Donatella Bradić, International Organization for Migration, Belgrade, Serbia, October 18, 2016.
7 Personal interview with Ivan Misković, Commissariat for Refugees, Belgrade, Serbia, October 20, 2016.
8 Personal interview with Nikola Kovačević, Belgrade Human Rights Center, Belgrade, Serbia, October 3, 2016.
9 Personal interview with Marta Stojić-Mitrović, Belgrade, Serbia, October 24, 2016.
10 Personal interview with Vesna Lukić, Institute of Social Sciences, Belgrade, Serbia, October 5, 2016.
11 Personal interview with Marta Stojić-Mitrović, Institute of Ethnography, Belgrade, Serbia, October 24, 2016.
12 Personal interview with Donatella Bradić and Marko Perović, Belgrade, Serbia, October 18, 2016.
13 Personal interview with official from international agency, Belgrade, Serbia, October 17, 2016.

References

Andreas, Peter. 2008. *Blue Helmets and Black Markets: The Business of Survival in the Siege of Sarajevo*. Ithaca: Cornell University Press.

Anon. 2015. "Temporary Center for Refugees, No Permanent Facilities." *B92*. Retrieved November 8, 2016 (www.b92.net/eng/news/politics.php?yyyy=2015&mm=09&dd=07&nav_id=95343).

Anon. 2016a. "Petronijević: Neophodne Izmene Postojećeg Zakona O Azilu. [Petronijević: Changes Needed to the Existing Laws on Asylum]." *RTS*. Retrieved October 3, 2016 (www.rts.rs/page/stories/sr/story/125/drustvo/2474314/petronijevic-zbog-priliva-migranata-neophodno-promeniti-zakon-o-azilu.html).

Anon. 2016b. "Pajtić: Dobro Je Da Vlast Širi Toleranciju Prema Iybeglicama. [Pajtic: It Is Good That the Government Is Promoting Tolerance towards Refugees]." *N1info.com*. Retrieved September 7, 2016 (http://rs.n1info.com/a134049/Vesti/Vesti/Pajtic-Dobro-je-da-vlast-siri-toleranciju-prema-izbeglicama.html).

Anon. 2016c. "Vulin: Serbia Must Be Equal to E.U. Members in Migrant Crisis." *Tanjug*. Retrieved November 8, 2016 (www.tanjug.rs/full-view_en.aspx?izb=274364).

Botić, Christiana. 2016. "Vanishing Act: The Disappearance of Refugee Aid in Serbia." *National Geographic*, November 30. Retrieved March 17, 2017 (http://voices.nationalgeographic.com/2016/11/30/vanishing-act-the-disappearance-of-refugee-aid-in-belgrade/).

Bracic, Ana. 2016. "Friend or Foe: Conflicting Identities Guiding Altruism." Paper presented at the American Political Science Association Annual Conference, September, Philadelphia, PA.

Centar za Slobodne Izbore i Demokratiju. 2013. "Public Perceptions of Discrimination in Serbia." Belgrade: Centar za Slobodne Izbore i Demokratiju.

Center for Insights in Survey Research. 2016. "Survey of Serbian Public Opinion: November 24–December 3, 2015." Belgrade: Center for Insights in Survey Research, International Republican Institute.

Collantes-Celador, Gemma and Ana E. Juncos. 2012. "The E.U. and Border Management in the Western Balkans: Preparing for European Integration or Safeguarding E.U. External Borders?" *Southeast European and Black Sea Studies* 12(2):201–20.

Damjanović, Milos. 2016. "Nations in Transit Country Report: Serbia." *Freedom House*. Retrieved September 7, 2016 (https://freedomhouse.org/sites/default/files/NiT2016%20Serbia_0.pdf).

Denti, Davide. 2015. "Serbia, the Unexpected Friend of Syrian Refugees on Their Way to Central Europe." Italy: Aspen Institute. Retrieved September 29, 2016 (www.aspeninstitute.it/aspenia-online/article/serbia-unexpected-friend-syrian-refugees-their-way-central-europe).

Djinović, Slobodan and Srdja Popović. 2015. "The Little Country Leading the Way in Europe's Refugee Crisis." *Slate.com*. Retrieved January 23, 2017 (www.slate.com/articles/news_and_politics/foreigners/2015/11/serbia_is_leading_the_way_in_europe_s_refugee_crisis_it_knows_what_is_needed.html).

Djokić, Dejan. 2015. "Wait, the Serbs Are Now the Good Guys?" *Open Democracy*. Retrieved October 10, 2016 (www.opendemocracy.net/can-europe-make-it/dejan-djokic/wait-serbs-are-now-good-guys).

Dveri. 2016. "Dveri: Government Not to Tell the Truth about Migrants." *Dveri*. Retrieved October 6, 2016 (https://dveri.rs/saopstenja/vlast-ne-sme-da-kaze-istinu-o-migrantima).

Entman, Robert M. 2004. *Projections of Power: Framing News, Public Opinion, and US Foreign Policy*. Chicago: University of Chicago Press.
European Union Delegation to Serbia. 2016. "How the E.U. Is Working with Serbia to Cope with Migration: Facts and Figures on E.U. Support." Retrieved October 20, 2016 (http://europa.rs/how-the-eu-is-working-with-serbia-to-cope-with-migration-facts-and-figures-on-eu-support/?lang=en).
Flanik, William. 2011. "'Bringing F.P.A. Back Home': Cognition, Constructivism, and Conceptual Metaphor." *Foreign Policy Analysis* 7(4):423–46.
Fosson, Gabriel. 2011. "The Serbian Government's Response to Human Trafficking." *European Journal of Crime, Criminal Law, and Criminal Justice* 19(3):183–98.
Freedom House. 2016. "Nations in Transit 2016." *Freedom House*. Retrieved September 9, 2016 (https://freedomhouse.org/report/nations-transit/nations-transit-2016).
Goffman, Erving. 1986. *Frame Analysis: An Essay on the Organization of Experience*. Boston: Northeastern University Press.
Greenhill, Kelly M. 2016. "Open Arms Behind Barred Doors: Fear, Hypocrisy and Policy Schizophrenia in the European Migration Crisis." *European Law Journal* 22(3):317–32.
InSerbia. 2016. "Vučić: Serbia Cannot Be E.U.'S Defence against Migrants." Retrieved October 9, 2016 (https://inserbia.info/today/2016/09/vucic-serbia-cannot-be-eus-defence-against-migrants/).
International Organization for Migration. 2016. "Europe/Mediterranean Migration Response." *International Organization for Migration*, September 22. Retrieved March 17, 2017 (www.iom.int/sitreps/europe-mediterranean-migration-crisis-response-situation-report-22-september-2016).
Ivanisević, Nenad. 2016. "Open Letter to International Humanitarian and Non-Governmental Organizations." Government of Serbia.
Jovanović, Igor. 2016. "Serbian Minister Bans Anti-Migrant Protests." *Balkan Insight*. Retrieved November 3, 2016 (www.balkaninsight.com/en/article/civil-sector-wows-ban-of-anti-migrants-protest-08-26-2015).
Jukić, Elvira. 2013. "Youth Emigration Causing Balkan 'Brain Drain'." *Balkan Insight*. Retrieved October 21, 2016 (www.balkaninsight.com/en/article/young-people-leave-serbia-bosnia-the-most).
Kogovšek Šalamon, Neža. 2016. "Asylum Systems in the Western Balkan Countries: Current Issues." *International Migration* 54(6):151–63.
Lakoff, George. 2009. *The Political Mind: A Cognitive Scientist's Guide to Your Brain and Its Politics*. New York: Penguin Books.
Lilyanova, Velina. 2016. "Briefing: Serbia's Role in Dealing with the Migration Crisis." Vol. PE 589.819. European Parliamentary Research Service.
Lindstrom, Nicole. 2007. "Transnational Responses to Human Trafficking: The Politics of Anti-Trafficking in the Balkans." Pp. 61–80 in H.R. Friman and Simon Reich, eds. *Human Trafficking, Human Security and the Balkans*. Pittsburgh: University of Pittsburgh Press.
Lukić, Vesna. 2016. "Understanding Transit Asylum Migration: Evidence from Serbia." *International Migration* 54(4):31–44.
Macdowall, Andrew. 2015. "Wait, the Serbs Are Now the Good Guys?" *Politico*. Retrieved October 11, 2016 (www.politico.eu/article/serbia-croatia-hungary-orban-migrants-schengen-crisis/).
Marinković, Lazara. 2017. "Refugees Stranded on Serbia-Hungary Border Amid Winter." *Al-Jazeera.com*. Retrieved January 24, 2017 (www.aljazeera.com/indepth/inpic

tures/2017/01/refugees-stranded-serbia-hungary-border-winter-170113161612570.html).
Miletić, Aleksandar R. 2013. "Serbia Vs. Europe." *Pescanik*. Retrieved October 21, 2016 (http://pescanik.net/serbia-vs-europe/).
Ministry of Foreign Affairs. n.d. "Diaspora." Retrieved October 21, 2016 (www.mfa.gov.rs/en/consular-affairs/diaspora/diaspora-general-information).
Nikitović, Vladimir and Vesna Lukić. 2010. "Could Refugees Have a Significant Impact on the Future Demographic Change of Serbia?" *International Migration* 48(1):106–28.
Nikolić, Drasko and Dusko Bodroža. 2012. "Positioning and Re-Positioning of National Brand of Serbia in Order to Increase to Increase Exports, Foreign Direct Investments and Tourism Development." Pp. 488–505 in João Andrade, Marta Simões, Ivan Stosić, Dejan Erić, and Hasan Hanić, eds. *Managing Structural Changes: Trends and Requirements*. Coimbra: Institute of Economic Sciences.
Ninamedia. 2015. "Serbian Citizens' Attitudes towards Asylum-Seekers/Migrants." Belgrade: Ninamedia Research. Retrieved February 28, 2017 (www.kirs.gov.rs/docs/aktuelno/Attitudes%20towards%20asylum%20seekers,%20May%202016.pdf).
Nova Srpska Politička Misao. 2016. "Srbija, Leto 2016." Belgrade: Nova Srpska Politička Misao. Retrieved November 8, 2016 (www.nspm.rs/istrazivanja-javnog-mnjenja/srbija-leto-2016.html).
Pantović, Milivoje. 2016. "Serbia Braces for Rise in Refugee Numbers." *Balkan Insight*. Retrieved August 31, 2016 (www.balkaninsight.com/en/article/serbia-is-expanding-capacaties-for-refugees-07-21-2016).
Pavlović, Aleksandar. 2016. "A Passage to Europe: Serbia and the Refugee Crisis." *Contemporary Southeastern Europe* 3(1):59–65.
Pupavac, Vanessa and Mladen Pupavac. 2015. "By Welcoming Syrian Refugees, Serbs Hope to Salvage Their Reputation." *The Conversation*. Retrieved January 24, 2017 (http://theconversation.com/by-welcoming-syrian-refugees-serbs-hope-to-salvage-their-reputation-47802).
Regional Cooperation Council. 2016. "Balkan Barometer 2016: Public Opinion Survey." Sarajevo: Regional Cooperation Council.
Statistical Office of the Republic of Serbia. 2012. "The Most Predominant Ethnic Communities in the Republic of Serbia." Retrieved October 21, 2016 (http://media.popis2011.stat.rs/2012/Presentation_Ethnicity.pdf).
Stojić-Mitrović, Marta. 2014. "Serbian Migration Policy Concerning Irregular Migration and Asylum in the Context of the E.U. Integration Process." *Issues in Ethnology and Anthropology* 9(4):1105–20.
Stojić-Mitrović, Marta and Ela Meh. 2016. "The Reproduction of Borders and the Contagiousness of Illegalisation: A Case of a Belgrade Youth Hostel." *Glasnik Etnografskog instituta S.A.N.U.* 63(3):623–38.
Subasić, Katarina. 2015. "Recalling Their War, Belgraders Embrace Syrian Refugees." Lebanon: Daily Star. Retrieved September 6, 2016 (www.dailystar.com.lb/News/Middle-East/2015/Aug-28/313065-recalling-their-war-belgraders-embrace-syrian-refugees.ashx?utm_source=Magnet&utm_medium=Entity%20page&utm_campaign=Magnet%20tools).
Tarrow, Sidney G. 2011. *Power in Movement: Social Movements and Contentious Politics*. Cambridge: Cambridge University Press.
Tarrow, Sidney G. 2013. *The Language of Contention: Revolutions in Words, 1688–2012*. Cambridge: Cambridge University Press.

U.S. Department of State. 2016. "Serbia." U.S. Department of State. Retrieved November 8, 2016 (www.state.gov/j/tip/rls/tiprpt/countries/2015/243523.htm).

Vujadinović, Snežana, Dejan Sabić, Marko Joksimović, Rajko Golić, Liljana Živkovic, and Dragica Gatarić. 2013. "Asylum Seekers from Serbia and the Problems of Returnees: Why Serbia Is among the World's Leading Countries in Number of Asylum Seekers." *Dve domovini* 37:53–69.

Weiss, Thomas G. and Amir Pasić. 1997. "Reinventing U.N.H.C.R.: Enterprising Humanitarians in the Former Yugoslavia 1991–1995." *Global Governance* 3(1):41–57.

3

FROM AMBIGUOUS REFUGEES TO POTENTIAL CITIZENS

Turkey's Domestic and International Challenges and Its Syrians

Sultan Tepe

UNIVERSITY OF ILLINOIS AT CHICAGO

Anahit Gomtsian

UNIVERSITY OF ILLINOIS AT CHICAGO
LAKE FOREST COLLEGE

> *Political and Military Sociology: An Annual Review*, 2017, Vol. 45: 36–53.

> *Described as the refugee capital of the world, Turkey's influx of refugees coincided with a consolidation of power within the ruling party, the introduction of an ambitious peace process with the Kurds, and a tumultuous relationship with the EU. Placing Turkey's policies into the broader regional context traces the transformation of Syrian refugees from "guests" to potential citizens. We examine the ways in which refugee-related practices are formed in Turkey and negotiated between Turkey and the EU by focusing on the interplay of a set of factors from the initial legal ambiguity of refugee status, the internationalization of the Syrian crisis, and the unwillingness of Western countries to admit displaced Syrians. Turning Syrian refugees into both burdens and strategic assets to the Turkish state with important implications for the country's democracy, the existing policies amount to the formation of a transnational precarity regime that focuses on the management of Syrians.*

Introduction

One-fifth of Syria's population has left the country since 2011, creating one of the most severe humanitarian crises of recent decades. Behind the crisis was the far-reaching impact of the Arab uprisings that were initiated by the Tunisian revolution of January 2011. Protests against the government erupted in the southern Syrian town of Deraa, leading to demands for President Bashar al-Assad's resignation. The government's violent crackdown against protesters pitted various Sunni groups that formed the sectarian majority against the President's Shia minority sect, rapidly escalating violent confrontations into a full-fledged civil war (Carpenter 2013). The internal turmoil, further exacerbated by regional conflicts among different ethnic and sectarian groups, gained an international dimension as the jihadist group Islamic State (IS) claimed territorial control and created an alternative to the disintegrating Syrian state. Reflecting the depth of the crisis, the United Nations estimates that more than 6 million Syrians are internally displaced and nearly five million have sought resettlement in neighboring countries (Migration Policy Center 2016).

Underlying the current analysis is the argument that what came to be known as "the Syrian refugee crisis" encompassed a web of intricate challenges that were caused by the sudden displacement of people to transit countries that had ambiguous refugee regimes as well as to final destination countries whose increasingly restrictive treatment of refugees has reduced them to a security threat. Offering a brief review of the regional refugee regime (or, rather, lack thereof) with a focus on Turkey's policies, this analysis questions how the interactions between domestically defined refugee status in the border countries and the increasing limitations on refugees by final destination countries interact, forming a transnational precarity status for Syrians.

More specifically, behind the Syrian humanitarian crisis lies the lack of a refugee regime in the region, where states adopt dual policies of acceptance, on the one hand, and exclusion, on the other, in an effort to balance humanitarian concerns as well as transnational and domestic power relations. Although the lack of clarity regarding refugee status puts the Syrian population in a more precarious position, an ambiguous legal framework also makes these initial entry, or transit, states important actors in negotiating policies with destination states. Indeed, the EU-Turkey agreement reveals that the fear of receiving a large number of Syrians created an environment in which the EU and Turkey institutionalized the treatment of Syrians in Turkey as temporary guests. Such agreements not only failed to address the basic as well as the long-term needs of Syrians, but they also reinforced their treatment as transnational precarities (i.e., populations living in conditions lacking in predictability, job security, material, and psychological welfare) (Agamben 1998).

When political and legal conditions are taken into account, Turkey's puzzling refugee policies stem from a rare geographical limitation in its acceptance of the 1951 Convention on Refugees, which assigns refugee status to only those who come to Turkey from a European home country. Those who arrive from outside Europe can remain in Turkey temporarily under the category of asylum seeker without gaining refugee status. This absence of a clearly defined refugee status reduces Syrians to subjects of the ruling party's policies and negotiations. Regionally, the impact of Turkey's conditional recognition of the 1951 Convention and its 1967 Protocol was exacerbated by Lebanon and Jordan's decision not to recognize the Convention at all. As a result, the states closest to Syria lack a well-defined domestic and regional legal framework regarding the acceptance and integration of refugees, in general, and the treatment of a mass arrival of refugees, in particular. On the other hand, while the EU and European states have a defined legal framework and refugee policy, they seek to limit access due to a host of factors, including increasing concerns about population balance, financial crises, security threats, and adverse public opinion. Indeed, large numbers of people in each European country, in some cases as high as 70 percent, view refugees from Syria as a major threat and unacceptable (Poushter 2016).

Against this regional backdrop, the following section explores how the distinct interests and policies in the region interact, forging a transnational precarity regime vis-à-vis the Syrian refugees. More specifically, an inquiry into both local conditions and international agreements highlights how the EU-Turkey Action Plan and the recent policy reforms adopted in Turkey to improve conditions for Syrian refugees have, on the one hand, created a number of contingent protections that improve certain conditions for the refugee population, while, on the other hand, amplifying certain existing disparities within that population and consolidating its role as a strategic population in domestic and transnational negotiations.

Contested Status: Syrians and Regional Refugee Policy

Whatever direction refugees choose to cross Syria's now-contested borders to avoid the impact of civil war, they find themselves in a highly complex legal environment. Although the 1951 Geneva Convention ensures that safe haven be provided to people fleeing persecution, it leaves open the question of who should provide that protection (as a "safe country of asylum"). As a result, asylum seekers are not able to go wherever they would prefer to settle, but are expected to instead remain in the *first* country they reach, where they will be offered protection. According to the 1951 Convention, such a "safe country" is expected to offer effective protection without the risk of return to the country of origin or another country where the asylum seeker may be subject to persecution—known as the *non-refoulement* obligation (UNHCR 1951/2010: 3). The recent influx of refugees into Europe revealed the complexity of the *non-refoulement* obligation with the emergence of EU policy that revisits the definition of "safe country." As such, EU policy permits the resettlement of asylum seekers to a "safe third country" if conditions there do not expose refugees to imminent threats to their life and liberty. For a country to be considered a "safe third country" for the asylum seeker, an individual evaluation is required and consideration must be given to whether an applicant's return to that country is reasonable, often based on family ties or previous residency (UNHCR 2016b). While organizations such as Amnesty International have questioned whether countries with increasingly volatile political environments, such as Turkey's, may be deemed "safe" under the legal definition, the increasing unwillingness of EU states to admit refugees has led to a less stringent definition of "safe country" (Amnesty International 2016b). This is evident by the fact that the EU's reports on the deteriorating democratic conditions of certain countries and its positive assessments of their "safety" for refugees yielded contradictory results (European Commission 2016a). Therefore, despite the legal classification, different assessments of the conditions within the "third country" can create another nebulous area where policies and the transfer of refugees become subject to political negotiation among EU states as well as between EU and non-EU countries.

At the regional level, it is not surprising that Turkey, Lebanon, and Jordan have received the highest number of Syrian refugees given their common borders with Syria (Amnesty International 2015). Indeed, Lebanon and Jordan combined are home to more than 1.6 million Syrian refugees (UNHCR 2017). Given previous waves of refugee arrivals, the total number of refugees (around a third of the total population) makes them the countries with the highest number of refugees per capita in the world (Lenner and Schmelter 2016). Yet, lacking a clear refugee policy, each country's treatment of Syrian refugees oscillates between permissiveness and exclusivity. For instance, although Syrians were registered through UNHCR in Lebanon, the registration ended in 2015 upon the state's adoption of the Policy Paper in October 2014 asserting that Lebanon contributed sufficiently to addressing the refugee crisis and adopting new criteria reducing the numbers of UNHCR registered Syrians in Lebanon (Dionigi 2016). Indeed, the country increasingly adopted a restive refugee policy due to the destabilizing impact of its recognition of Palestinians as refugees in 1969 and the internal turmoil caused by population movement amongst clashing ethnic, religious, and sectarian groups. As such, Lebanon, which has historically maintained an open door policy to refugees, does not grant any refugee status and treats Syrians as temporary residents (Saliba 2016). Facing financial pressures and violent attacks, the country has also gradually instituted stricter border controls and push-backs to Syria (Aziz 2016). Indeed, President Aoun, who was elected in October 2016, took an anti-refugee platform to a new level, calling for the need to return refugees to their country of origin regardless of the status of conflict there (Francis and Khaledi 2015; Fiddlan-Qasmiyeh 2017).

Likewise, with a *de facto* open door policy, Jordan received more than 1.4 million refugees, reaching 11 percent of its population (Lenner and Schmelter 2016:122). Attesting to the importance of international institutions' ability to contribute to the improvement of the legal environment, the UNHCR registered more than 650,000 Syrians as refugees in Jordan by the summer of 2016. Previously, in 2014, the government released the National Resilience Plan (NRP) to mitigate the effects of the Syrian crisis on Jordan and host communities. As noted in the report, although the lack of language barriers made the Jordanian system more accessible to Syrians, Jordan's limited infrastructure and the large scale of the Syrian resettlement project led to a crisis in the provision of health and educational services (Ministry of Planning and International Cooperation, Jordan 2014). Moreover, allegations that Syrians were taking locals' jobs led to tighter labor market enforcement, in which Syrians could be sent back to a refugee camp or deported altogether if they were found without job permits. To avoid such risks, many decided to work at night or to send children to work instead (Lenner and Schmelter 2016). By mid-2016, Jordan closed its border with Syria, citing security concerns and effectively stranding refugees at the border.

Following in the footsteps of this regional pattern—one of moving from free to restrictive refugee entry, Turkey also adopted a stricter policy and even initiated the construction of a concrete wall along its border. Scheduled for completion in 2019, the 3-meter high and 900 kilometer- long wall is presented as the third-longest wall in the world with the potential of drastically altering movement and interactions across the border and, thus, the entry of refugees (Butler and Coskun 2016).

In short, the inability of Syrians to obtain refugee status, particularly in Turkey, and their assignment as short-term "guests," contributes to their geographical dispersion. While 10 percent of refugees live in border camps, the rest live alongside Turkish locals in urban and rural settings. As in Jordan and Lebanon, the lack of refugee status and poor registration practices results in a wide range of problems. Moreover, Disaster and Emergency Management Presidency (AFAD) surveys indicate that only 20 percent of Syrians have a secondary education, resulting in competition with locals for employment in low-skilled markets and for the few economic opportunities available (AFAD 2013).

Turkey's Syrians: Domestic Challenges

Turkey's open door policy has rendered it the "refugee capital of the world" and a pivotal actor in the Syrian crisis. Bereft of the full legal protection of refugee status, 2.8 million Syrian refugees are registered under "temporary protection" (UNHCR 2017:28). Such treatment is consistent with the country's legal structure, which presumes that Turkey is a transit country rather than a final destination for Syrians. Reflecting this status, Syrian refugees were until recently described as "guests" in official state discourse.

Despite their treatment as "guests," the sheer number of Syrians entering Turkey over a short period of time following the historic rapprochement between Syria and Turkey rendered the "refugee crisis" as the most important and divisive issue facing the country. Behind the strong reactions were the Turkish government's strong anti-Assad stance and its commitment to promote regime change, as well as the unexpected escalation of the conflict into a full-fledged civil war and the dramatically increasing number of Syrians fleeing the conflict. This led to the division in public opinion. For instance, a 2013 survey conducted by Kadir Has University (HAS Data 2013) showed that 36.3 percent of those polled endorsed the idea that "the influx of refugees should be stopped and that previously arrived refugees should be sent back." A significant number (39 percent) also believed that the government should not get involved in any conflict within an Arab country. Meanwhile, hostility towards the EU and potential Turkish membership grew. Other surveys noted that more than 77 percent of respondents believed that the EU was not sincere in its negotiation efforts (i.e., it did not intend to accept Turkey as a member), and 37 percent of respondents rejected EU membership (HAS Data 2013). This intersection of attitudes regarding Syrian refugees and perceived EU antipathy towards Turkey created an environment in which the ruling Justice and Democracy Party (JDP) began to reconsider its international policies and to deal with the impact of its Syrian policy domestically, rather than multilaterally. Thus, pressure from its own population as well as the protracted nature of the Syrian civil war led to the formulation of certain new policies and an increasing tolerance of informal solutions in a range of areas, from labor market to education reform.

Syrian Access to the Turkish Labor Market

To understand the labor conditions for Syrians in Turley, a brief review of the country's labor market is necessary. In the southeast provinces where Syrian refugees are concentrated, the unemployment rate is nearly three times higher than the overall Turkish average, in some places reaching as high as 50 percent (Grisgraber and Hollingsworth 2016:4–5). In this job market marked by high unemployment and low skills, many Syrians report that despite their efforts they cannot compete with locals in the more widely accessible professions, such as cab-driving, which also often present high licensing and maintenance fees. The AFAD report indicates that since 80 percent of Syrians do not have a secondary level education, the inclusion of 1.4 million Syrians into the labor market during a time of recession in Turkey, amounts to the expansion of the country's labor force by 5 percent in areas that require low-skilled labor (World Bank 2015; Del Carpio 2015; Organization for Economic Cooperation and Development 2016a, 2016b). Moreover, it is also important to note that even those Syrians who arrive in Turkey with some financial capacity are usually not well positioned to maintain their socioeconomic status due to general unstable economic conditions.

In addition to such economic uncertainty, the impact of the failed coup in late 2016 led to a further deterioration in an fragile national economy, resulting in an overall economic slowdown and even the possibility of a future negative growth rate (Organization for Economic Cooperation and Development 2016a, 2016b; Sonmez 2016). Moreover, while generally receiving only about half the standard salary paid to Turkish citizens, Syrians are enmeshed in an exploitative work market (Grisgraber and Hollingsworth 2016). While certain skilled jobs favor locals over refugees, widely accepted practices of hiring unregistered labor drives wages down for both locals and refugees. Thus, for example, while an increase in demand for housing led to an increase in the construction of new homes, and thus the number of construction jobs, the overall effect of more migrants was to lower average wages. Indeed, before the arrival of Syrian refugees, locals reported having received more than five times the current salary rate (ORSAM 2015).

At the same time, despite falling wages in areas populated heavily by refugees, people also report a sharp increase in rents and prices for local produce. Thus, while the lack of formal labor market integration can be attributed to the nature and demand of such markets, Syrian refugees are further impeded not only by limited skill sets but also by stringent registration requirements with geographical restrictions, quotas, high employment registration fees, and intricate paperwork needed to access the formal labor market (Lenner and Schmelter 2016). In short, then, while the influx of Syrians has led to some positive contributions (such as the transfer of investment from Syria to Turkey, which has increased the number of Syrian firms three-fold by bringing in a 4 million-dollar investment), such positive impact remains regional and limited (Kirisci 2014; ORSAM 2015). Instead, these changes have created local economies where refugees simultaneously create an advantage (e.g., higher rents and cheaper labor for small business) as well as disadvantages for locals (e.g., lower wages for unskilled and seasonal workers), thereby creating highly complex and contentious social and economic micro-regimes.

Amidst new domestic reforms aimed at existing and incoming Syrian refugees, new regulations on work permits were adopted in January of 2016, expanding the labor rights for certain groups. The Law on Work Permits for Foreigners (No. 4817) presents a welcoming attitude, especially towards skilled migrant workers. However, work permits are rather rare and are tied to employers who must apply on behalf of employees. The temporary status also requires residency in their city of registration, and the number of total refugees in a workplace cannot exceed 10 percent of the local workforce. In addition, whether a Turkish citizen is available for the same position is taken into account prior to granting the permit. Thus, with formal access restricted amid a limited number of jobs, between January and April 2016 only 2000 Syrians applied for permission to work (Fiddlan-Qasmiyeh 2017). Thus, notwithstanding the official recognition of some labor rights, labor competition remains very intense, overall national market conditions unpredictable, and state-sponsored social aid to retrain Syrians is limited. Indeed, reports indicate that Turkey's work permit program may only benefit 10 percent of Syrians (Grisgraber and Hollingsworth 2016).

These conditions of the Turkish labor market and the concomitant economic insecurities to which they lead also have a number of international consequences. For example, the generous monthly allowance offered to refugees by countries like Sweden proves enormously attractive to refugees. As a result, the more established and attainable legal and economic securities in other countries increase the desire of many refugees to move to countries such as Sweden and Germany at any cost. However, limitations on legal passage, in turn, forge a highly lucrative human trafficking sector, where refugees are charged $1,500 on average to be taken from Turkey to Greece. Considering Turkey's limited infrastructure to meet the demands of Syrian refugees, such transfers are not always discouraged.

Syrian Access to Education in Turkey

Another striking indicator of Turkey's limited infrastructure is its inability to meet the needs of young Syrians. Of the total number of Syrian refugees within

Turkey, more than half are children. At the same time, the United Nations International Children's Emergency Fund (UNICEF) estimates that nearly 80 percent of these children are not attending school (Kingsley 2016a). Although some reports indicate that 64,000 Syrian students were able to attend schools with a rather favorable student to teacher ratio, given that 10 percent of the population lives in camps, such numbers fail to illustrate the lack of educational opportunities at large (Emin 2016). In fact, some surveys indicate that around 80 percent of families prefer to put their children into the labor market to help subsidize family income. Because Syrian refugees do not have automative, legal labor market access, as indicated previously, employers often pay less than minimum wage, driving reluctant parents to send their children to work, rather than to school (Kingsley 2016a). Indeed, despite the fact that the Turkish legal framework grants children the right to attend school, EU commission reports draw attention to the institutionalization of a vicious cycle of poverty among Syrians in light of protracted displacement, limited local capacities, language barriers, geographical distance, as well as socioeconomic barriers (sometimes leading to the recourse of child labor and early marriage) that prevent a large number of refugee children from receiving any formal education (European Commission 2016d; Human Rights Watch 2016).

The school-age Syrian population constitutes around 5 percent of the more than 16 million children enrolled in Turkey's public schools (based on 2014–15 figures), yet language barriers require the creation of special renovated schools with Syrian "volunteer" teachers, leading to a 30 percent increase in the number of children in school in 2015 over the previous year, yet still representing only 13 percent of school age students. In pre-conflict Syria, secondary and lower secondary school enrollments were 99 percent and 82 percent, respectively, with a high degree of gender parity (UNHCR 2016a). The low number of students attending school in Turkey, however, can be traced to Syrian families not having residency registration, non-compliance of local schools in admitting Syrian students, an inability to understand the Turkish language, maltreatment of children, and the lack of sufficient income (Gee 2016). The impact of limited educational opportunities is exacerbated by a large number of micro-factors, such as difficulties in determining the proper grade level, a failure to address language skills since all public schools require Turkish, and a changing work environment that compels refugees to re-settle as seasonal workers or in low-skilled jobs.

Due to constant relocation and limited availability of education, many consider the current Syrian generation a "lost generation." International campaigns such as "No to Lost Generation," which are trying to address issues of education, note that 67 percent of Syrians live in poverty or extreme poverty. National governments that respond to the educational needs of Syrian children by opening public schools are not equipped with a curriculum that addresses the refugee populations' needs (UNHCR 2017). As a result, growing numbers of child laborers and low school enrollment rates are creating a generation ill-equipped to enter the service-oriented markets or capable of contributing to the development of a strong democratic state (Lipset 1959: 79; Przeworski et al. 2000).

The Social Integration of Syrians

Although Syrians are often treated as a monolithic group, in reality they are quite diverse, divided not only by socioeconomic status but also by their linguistic, ethnic, and religious identities. The internal divisions that destabilized Syria have far-reaching effects. In refugee camps, for example, tension often run high between those who are for or against the Assad regime as well as those from different Islamic sects (Dağlıoğlu 2014). Moreover, despite acknowledging the tragic conditions of Syrians and the necessity of providing humanitarian aid, a very small percentage of Turks (17 percent) express feeling any "cultural affinity" with Syrian refugees (Erdoğan 2014). For their part, too, Syrian refugees reveal that the difficulty they face in learning the Turkish language as well as the lack of access to public services are significant barriers to integration (Yıldız and Uzgören 2016:10).

As such, the social integration of Syrian refugees depends largely on their proximity to the dominant identity of local groups. For example, Kurdish groups are more receptive to Kurdish-Syrians yet more skeptical towards Arab-Syrians (ORSAM 2015). Furthermore, while Syrians with high socioeconomic status move to large cities, those with limited means stay in the regions closer to the border. In places where the Syrian population exceeds the local population, like Reyhanli and Kilis, integration poses even more problems. While Turks number 60,000 in Reyhanli, the Syrian population amounts to 100,000. Thus, the city has been dubbed "Little Syria" (Anderson 2013). Similarly, Syrians exceed the local population in Kilis. In such places, many local Turks have left due to security concerns, leading to the formation of such Syrian dominant towns (Kırmızitaş et al. 2016).

Another contributing challenge to social integration is the incidents of violence that are attributed to Syrian-based groups, easily spiraling into resentment and rejection of Syrians. In Gaziantep, a group of 25 Syrians was removed from a neighborhood after an altercation turned violent (Burun 2014). Such incidents have led to a hardening of anti-Syrian attitudes. Even Turkish citizens who express hospitality and social acceptance towards Syrians on humanitarian grounds hold that Syrians are "guests" and should eventually return to their country (Yıldız and Uzgören 2016:11). However, despite the discursive appeal of a "temporal stay" as "guests," it is likely that at least 65 percent of Syrians will remain in Turkey after the war concludes (Aras and Yasun 2016). Thus, the disconnect between reality and the official discourse of temporality serves to thwart any discussion on long-term issues. Thus, newspapers that carry titles such as "Syrians Won't Return," are surprising to their readers (e.g., Çamlıbel 2016). Perhaps due to this common perception—one reinforced by official discourse—President Erdoğan's statements in July 2016 and later in January 2017 that qualified Syrians (especially those with high professional skills) would be granted full citizenship evoked a range of often negative reactions (BBC Türkçe 2017). Objections have ranged from the financial burden that such inclusion would bring about to the argument that the proposal to turn refugees into voters was a form of political advantage (Karakis 2016).

The result of such economic and social challenges has been to lead many Syrian refugees to turn towards Europe for resettlement. Indeed, nearly one million refugees requested asylum in Europe between April 2011 and October 2016, with Germany and Sweden being the most requested host states within the EU (UNHCR 2016c). Yet despite the existence of a more developed institutional infrastructure and better economic conditions, European governments have expressed reluctance (and, in some cases, overt objection) to accepting or integrating Syrian refugees (Frej 2015). In short, global economic challenges, the Eurozone debt crisis, Britain's vote to leave the EU, security concerns, and anti-immigrant sentiments in Europe have generated an environment that is not conducive to refugees, with countries instead turning to stricter border controls.

National Impasses and Regional Solutions—the Turkey–EU Action Plan

The images of sinking and overloaded boats in the Aegean Sea became the face of widespread human smuggling to Europe (Human Rights Watch 2015). As argued earlier, perceived and existing disparities in the legal and economic conditions between EU and non-EU countries created a persistent demand among refugees to move to a designated safe country. So strong has been this demand that a research study by the EU's law enforcement body found that, of 1,500 asylum seekers, refugees, and economic migrants surveyed, 90 percent had paid a criminal gang to help them reach Europe (McDonald-Gibson 2016). Increased severity of punishment (e.g., an increase in prison sentences from 3 to 8 years for smuggling) has not deterred smugglers, and fewer than 200 people were arrested in 2015, despite the routine passage of smuggled migrants from Turkey to other countries.

As part of the effort to stop the influx of Syrians into Europe, in late 2015 the EU entered into an agreement with Turkey—the Joint Action Plan—whereby migrants arriving on the Greek islands are to be deported back to Turkey. The Plan aims to step "up cooperation on support of Syrians under temporary protection and migration management in a coordinated effort to address the crisis created by the situation in Turkey" (European Commission 2015). With oversight from the European Commission and the Turkish government, the Plan seeks to support Syrians who are placed under "temporary protection" and strengthen cooperation in order to prevent "irregular migration" (European Commission 2015).

At first glance, the agreement appears to be geared towards helping refugees receive better information regarding refugee status and the possibilities for settlement. It is also aimed at assisting Turkey in combatting migrant smuggling through enhanced communication networks and financial assistance, to revitalize its EU accession negotiations, and to develop a visa liberalization dialog with the EU. Among other things, the agreement offers assistance to strengthen the capacity of the Turkish Coast Guard, largely in relation to surveillance, to enhance cooperation with Bulgarian and Greek authorities in order to prevent irregular migration across common land borders, and to ensure that asylum procedures are completed in a timely manner by ensuring that refugee status is granted without delay (European Commission 2016c). Although the Plan was criticized for bartering refugee rights in return for visa liberalization, for many the legal issue was the EU's designation of Turkey as a safe final destination country despite stipulations in the Geneva Convention requiring careful assessment of domestic conditions (Dutch Council for Refugees and European Council on Refugees and Exiles 2016.)

Whether or not, and to what extent, the EU-Turkey agreement has led to a substantial decline in the transition of refugees to Europe is contested. However, the Plan has institutionalized a transnational precarity regime in regards to Syrian refugees in several ways. First, while committing itself to mobilize new funds to support Turkey in its absorption of Syrian refugees, the Plan also *de facto* normalizes Turkey's treatment of refugees under "temporary protection" status and recognizes the country as a final destination country. However, as alluded to previously, "temporary protection status" does not address the reality of Syrian refugees who are likely to remain in Turkey long-term. More importantly, the status of "temporality" allows the government to decide on the scope and nature of rights granted to refugees without accountability to the refugee population or the international community. Second, as the agreement requires Turkey to implement policies facilitating refugee access to public services, it has the effect of reducing refugee-related issues to a question of creating a stronger migration *management* strategy. The focus on management, in turn, overshadows the need to develop a more comprehensive approach (Centre for Transnational Development and Collaboration 2015). Third, while as an EU candidate, Turkey is required to further develop its record of democracy and human rights, its judicial system, and treatment of minorities, the Plan compartmentalizes the treatment of Turkey. That is, by granting Turkey "safe third country" status, the EU is relieved of the pressure of receiving more refugees but has now created an evaluation of the human rights condition in Turkey that contradicts its own progress reports and the findings of some major democracy indices that confirm the country's deteriorating position on such indicators as civil liberties, free access to information, and freedom of expression (European Commission 2016a; Freedom House 2016).

In fact, a review of the EU's own evaluations—such as statements by the European Parliament—warn against the consolidation of this duality. The EU's negotiations with Turkey presume the country's ability to take in Syrian refugees and, thus, create two parallel tracks. The first track involves the EU's negotiations regarding Turkish membership. It is important to note that Turkey became an official EU candidate in 1999 and was asked to introduce a significant set of reforms to achieve full membership. The most recent EU Progress report calls for further urgent reforms and the modification of certain key institutions (e.g., independence of the judiciary), better treatment of the political opposition, and the implementation of anti-terrorism law (European Commission 2016a). Among other lists of "serious concerns" the report argues that "due process, the right to fair trial and the respect of the principle of the presumption of innocence should be guaranteed" (European Commission 2016a:72). In the same vein, recent statements from MEPs condemn violations of freedom of speech in Turkey—especially the intimidation of journalists—and call for a ceasefire in southeast Turkey and the resumption of the Kurdish peace process.

The EU's negotiations with Turkey over the refugee crisis constitute the second track. The Joint Action Plan primarily seeks to limit the number of refugees in Europe and promises to alleviate Turkish concerns regarding its capacity to accommodate Syrian refugees, while at the same time encouraging Turkey to make certain reforms and offering some benefits as reward. While the Plan is not to be taken as one of the requirements for full EU membership, it does include the promise of visa-free travel to the EU for Turkish citizens (European Commission 2016b). Moreover, a close review of the EU and Turkey discussions reveal that this second track set aside documented concerns regarding Turkish democracy to focus on Turkey's role in the refugee crisis, while asserting that "EU-Turkey cooperation on migration should not be linked to the calendar, content, and conditionality of the negotiation process" (European Parliament 2016). Such compartmentalization of the accession process from the refugee issue is significant, as the EU's negotiation and conditionality strategy for membership rests on the idea of "reinforcement by reward" (Schimmelfennig et al. 2003).

While the government of Turkey seeks to compartmentalize the issue of accession from that of refugees, the EU effectively undermines its warnings about Turkey's "state of emergency" and its problematic respect for human rights by declaring Turkey safe for refugees. Moreover, drastic changes in the composition of its security forces render implementation of some policies (e.g., the capture and return of smugglers and refugees) rather difficult (Kingsley 2016b). Revealing increasing discomfort with this duality, the European Parliament's call to suspend negotiations with Turkey and its unwillingness to extend visa-free travel to Turkish citizens risks termination of the Plan (Winter 2016). Pro-democratic groups in Turkey that have conventionally aligned themselves with the EU are disheartened. Already, only 15.3 percent of Turkish citizens believe that the EU is conducting Turkey's accession negotiations in an honest and fair way, and seven out of ten respondents believe membership is purposefully being prevented (HAS Data 2013).

It is important to note that the Syrian crisis and the Action Plan have taken place in a volatile context. The country's unexpected peace negotiations with the Kurdish groups, including the PKK, unsettled its conventional stance, and its relations with EU grew more strained. Although EU membership once had a very high level of support among the Turkish population, by 2013 only 42.4 percent of respondents supported Turkey's membership bid, and 47.6 percent believed that the EU did not intend to grant Turkey full membership. According to the same survey, 75 percent of respondents deemed Turkey's foreign policy as unsuccessful or partially successful, and the idea of a "privileged partnership with the EU" was supported by only 32.4 percent of respondents. By contrast, nearly 75 percent of respondents endorsed the idea of renewing diplomatic and economic relations with other countries (HAS Data 2013). Later, the EU and Turkey's Action Plan seemed to confirm the view that the EU could choose to ignore human rights violations when such treatment served its own interests. Even international groups described the EU's designation of Turkey as a safe third country as showing "a blithe disregard for international law," lowering Turkish public confidence in the EU to an all-time low (Amnesty International 2016a).

Conclusion

The Syrian refugee crisis in Turkey demonstrates that refugee management is not a national but a transnational issue. In that regard, the influx of refugees to Turkey and their treatment by the Turkish government and the EU cannot be seen as an exception. This case reveals the need for a transnational model. The reluctance to grant internationally protected refugee status by neighboring countries and the increasing tendency to seal borders confines Syrians to a gray zone of legal status. Existing indicators of global freedom designate Turkey and Lebanon as partly free and Jordan as not free, all with widely recognized low levels of political rights and civil liberties (Freedom House 2016). Given the economic and political insecurities characterizing these countries, their designation as "safe final countries" by international agreements reinforces the legally tenuous positions of refugees who are caught between a failed regime at home and highly volatile "safe" environments in their new countries of resettlement. Therefore, when approached from a transnational perspective, while power seems to lie in the hands of border states/transit countries, the policies and agreements of the final destination countries play a major role in determining the domestic treatment of refugees. The strategic agreement of refugee-averse but more stable final destination countries not only legitimizes the neighboring countries' treatment of refugees under "temporary" status but also undermines the undertaking of large scale and costly incentives to address the refugees' long-term needs. Such transnational regimes do not occur haphazardly, as this analysis shows. Instead, overlapping national interests interact to form a regime in which Syrians are the subjects of many negotiations without having a say in their formulations.

Existing policies—from contingent labor rights to insufficient investment in the education of children to overcome linguistic limitations and social barriers—suggest that the existing agreements and the Action Plan amount to a transnational precarity regime where uncertainties and insecurities about labor market and social well-being are not addressed but, rather, are *de facto* institutionalized.

Capturing the expansion of the newly forming transnational precarity regime, Chancellor Angela Merkel indicated that "we either have to let people come to us, or we have to combat the root causes of migration so that people see prospects for staying there, close to their homes" (Martin and Shalal 2016). Although they may appear as panacea, the emerging transnational precarity regimes fall short in offering comprehensive solutions to ever more pressing security, economic, and democratic concerns by strengthening states' reliance on informal and unregulated processes, institutions, and agencies in addressing the long-term needs of refugee communities.

References

AFAD (Disaster and Emergency Management Presidency, Republic of Turkey). 2013. "Syrian Refugees in Turkey 2013: Results of Field Research." Retrieved February 21, 2017 (https://data2.unhcr.org/en/documents/download/40157).

Agamben, Giorgio. 1998. *Homo Sacer: Sovereign Power and Bare Life*. Stanford, CA: Stanford University Press.

Amnesty International. 2015. "Syria's Refugee Crisis in Numbers." Retrieved February 21, 2017 (www.amnesty.org/en/latest/news/2015/09/syrias-refugee-crisis-in-numbers/).

Amnesty International. 2016a. "Amnesty International Press Release: Turkey-Illegal Mass Return of Syrian Refugees Expose Fatal Flaws in EU-Turkey Deal." April 1. Retrieved February 19, 2017 (www.amnesty.org/en/press- releases/2016/04/turkey-illegal-mass-returns-of-syrian-refugees-expose-fatal-flaws-in-eu-turkey-deal).

Amnesty International. 2016b. "No Safe Refuge: Asylum Seekers and Refugees Denied Effective Protection in Turkey." June 3. Retrieved February 21, 2017 (www.amnesty.org/en/documents/eur44/3825/2016/en).

Anderson, Gaia. 2013. "Little Syria." *Deutsche Welle*. Retrieved February 21, 2017 (www.dw.com/en/little-syria/g-16749325).

Aras, Bülent and Salih Yasun. 2016. "The Educational Opportunities and Challenges of Syrian Refugee Students in Turkey: Temporary Education Centers and Beyond." July. IPC Mercator Policy Brief. Istanbul Policy Center-Sabancı University-Stiftung Mercator Initiative.

Aziz, Jean. 2016. "Lebanon Reels under Weight of Syrian Refugee Crisis." *Al-Monitor*. (www.al-monitor.com/pulse/originals/2016/07/al-qaa-bombings-syrian-refugees-lebanon-reactions.html).

BBC Türkçe. 2017. "Erdoğan: Suriyeli ve Iraklıların bir kısmını vatandaşlığa alacağız. [Erdogan: We Will Admit a Certain Group of Iraqis and Syrians to Citizenship]." January 6. Retrieved February 21, 2017 (www.bbc.com/turkce/haberler-turkiye-38534106).

Burun, Eyyüp. 2014. "Gaziantep'te 25 Suriyeli gerginlik yaşanan mahalleden tahliye edildi. [25 Syrians Were Removed from the Neighborhood in Gaziantep]." *Hurriyet*. Retrieved February 19, 2017. (www.hurriyet.com.tr/gaziantepte-25-suriyeli-gerginlik-yasanan-mahalleden-tahliye-edildi-26724979).

Butler, Daren and Orhan Coskun. 2016. "Turkey to Complete Syria Border Wall within 5 Months, Official Says." *Reuters*, September 28. Retrieved February 21, 2017 (www.reuters.com/article/us-mideast-crisis-syria-turkey-idUSKCN11Y1MB).

Çamlibel, Cansu. 2016. "Suriyeliler Kalıcı. [Syrians Are Permanent]." *Hurriyet*. (www.hurriyet.com.tr/suriyeliler-kalici-40072604).

Carpenter, Ted Galen. 2013. "Tangled Web: The Syrian Civil War and Its Implications." *Mediterranean Quarterly* 24(1):1–11.

Centre for Transnational Development and Collaboration. 2015. "Syrian Refugees in Turkey, Gender Analysis." Retrieved February 21, 2017 (http://ctdc.org/analysis.pdf).

Dağlıoğlu, Emre Can. 2014. "10 soruda 'Suriyeli mülteciler' meselesi. [The 'Syrian Refugees' Issue in Ten Questions]." July 30. Retrieved February 21, 2017 (http://t24.com.tr/haber/10-soruda-suriyeli-multeciler-meselesi,266061).

Del Carpio, Ximena V. 2015. "The Impact of Syrian Refugees on the Turkish Labor Market." World Bank Policy Research Working Paper 7402. Retrieved February 21, 2017 (http://documents.worldbank.org/curated/en/505471468194980180/pdf/WPS7402.pdf).

Dionigi, Filippo. 2016. "The Syrian Refugee Crisis in Lebanon: State Fragility and Social Resilience." *London School of Economics Middle East Centre Paper Series*. Retrieved February 21, 2017 (http://eprints.lse.ac.uk/65565/1/Dionigi_Syrian_Refugees%20in%20Lebanon_Author_2016.pdf).

Dutch Council for Refugees and European Council on Refugees and Exiles. 2016. "The DCRE/ECRE Desk Research on Application of a Safe Third Country and a First Country of Asylum Concepts to Turkey." Retrieved February 21, 2017 (www.asylumlawdatabase.eu/sites/www.asylumlawdatabase.eu/files/aldfiles/turkey-note%20final%20edited%20DCR%20ECRE.pdf).

Emin, Muberra Nur. 2016. "Turkiye'Deki SuriYeli Cocuklarin Egitimi. [The Education of Syrian Children in Turkey]." *SETA*. (http://file.setav.org/Files/Pdf/20160309195808_turkiyedeki-suriyeli-cocuklarin-egitimi-pdf.pdf).

Erdoğan, M. Murat. 2014. "Perceptions of Syrians in Turkey." *Insight Turkey* 16(4):65–75.

European Commission. 2015. "EU-Turkey Joint Action Plan." October 15. Retrieved February 21, 2017 (http://europa.eu/rapid/press-release_MEMO-15-5860_en.htm).

European Commission. 2016a. "EC Turkey Report." Retrieved February 21, 2017 (https://ec.europa.eu/neighbourhood-enlargement/sites/near/files/pdf/key_documents/2016/20161109_report_turkey.pdf).

European Commission. 2016b. "European Commission Fact Sheet: Implementing the EU-Turkey Statement: Questions and Answers." Retrieved February 21, 2017 (http://europa.eu/rapid/press-release_MEMO-16-1664_en.htm).

European Commission. 2016c. "EU-Turkey Joint Action Plan: Implementation Report." Retrieved February 21, 2017 (https://ec.europa.eu/home-affairs/sites/homeaffairs/files/what-we-do/policies/european-agenda-migration/background-information/docs/eu_turkey_joint_action_plan_implementation_report_20160304_en.pdf).

European Commission. 2016d. "Humanitarian Implementation Plan for Turkey." June 2. Retrieved February 21, 2017 (http://ec.europa.eu/echo/sites/echo-site/files/hip_turkey_2016.pdf).

European Parliament. 2016. "Turkey: Need of Urgent Reforms in Key Areas, Say MEPs." *European Parliament News: Press Release*. Retrieved February 21, 2017 (www.europarl.europa.eu/news/en/news-room/20160407IPR21789/turkey-need-of-urgent-reforms-in-key-areas-say-meps).

Fiddlan-Qasmiyeh, Elena. 2017. "Syrian Refugees in Turkey, Jordan and Lebanon Face an Uncertain 2017." *The Conversation*, January 3. Retrieved February 21, 2017 (http://theconversation.com/syrian-refugees-in-turkey-jordan-and-lebanon-face-an-uncertain-2017–70747).

Francis, Pia and Hanan Khaledi. 2015. "Aoun Warns of Conspiracy to Settle Syrian Refugees in Lebanon." *Daily Star Lebanon News*, September 15. Retrieved February 21, 2017 (www.dailystar.com.lb/News/Lebanon-News/2015/Sep-15/315335-aoun-warns-of-conspiracy-to-settle-syrian-refugees-in-lebanon.ashx).

Freedom House. 2016. "Freedom House Report: Freedom in the World." Retrieved February 21, 2017 (https://freedomhouse.org/sites/default/files/FH_FITW_Report_2016.pdf).

Frej, Willa. 2015. "Here Are the European Countries That Want to Refuse Refugees." *The World Post*, September 9. Retrieved February 21, 2017 (www.huffingtonpost.com/entry/europe-refugees-not-welcome_us_55ef3dabe4b093be51bc8824).

Gee, Stephanie. 2016. "When I Picture My Future, I See Nothing." *Human Rights Watch*, November 8. Retrieved February 21, 2017 (www.hrw.org/report/2015/11/08/when-i-picture-my-future-i-see-nothing/barriers-education-syrian-refugee-children).

Grisgraber, Daryll and Ann Hollingsworth. 2016. "Planting the Seeds of Success? Turkey's New Refugee Work Permits." *Refugees International*, April 13. Retrieved February 21, 2017 (www.refugeesinternational.org/reports/2016/4/14/turkey).

HAS Data. 2013. Data translated from "Turk Dis Politikasi Kamuoyu Algilari Arasstirmasi. [Turkish Foreign Policy Public Perception Data]." Kadir Has Universitesi.

Human Rights Watch. 2015. "Europe's Refugee Crisis: An Agenda for Action." November 16. Retrieved February 21, 2017 (www.hrw.org/report/2015/11/16/europes-refugee-crisis/agenda-action).

Human Rights Watch. 2016. "Education for Syrian Refugee Children: What Donors and Host Countries Should Do." September. Retrieved February 21, 2017 (www.hrw.org/sites/default/files/supporting_resources/education_for_syrian_refugee_children_what_donors_and_host_countries_should_do.pdf0).

Karakis, Gizem. 2016. "Cumhurbaşkanı Erdoğan'dan Suriyeli sığınmacılara vatandaşlık mesajı. [Erdogan's Citizenship Message to Syrians]." *Hurriyet*, July 3. Retrieved February 21, 2017 (www.hurriyet.com.tr/cumhurbaskani-erdogandan-suriyeli-gocmenlere-vatandaslik-mesaji-40127078).

Kingsley, Patrick. 2016a. "From War to Sweatshop for Syria's Child Refugees." *The Guardian*, May 6. Retrieved February 21, 2017 (www.theguardian.com/world/2016/may/06/war-to-sweatshop-for-child-refugees).

Kingsley, Patrick. 2016b. "Turkish Police Withdrawal from Greece Stalls EU Migration Pact." *The Guardian*, August 31. Retrieved February 21, 2017 (www.theguardian.com/world/2016/aug/31/turkish-police-withdrawal-greece-stalls-eu-migration-pact-unhcr).

Kirisci, Kemal. 2014. "Syrian Refugees and Turkey's Challenges: Going beyond Hospitality." *The Brookings Institute*, May 14. Retrieved February 21, 2017 (www.brookings.edu/wp-content/uploads/2016/06/Syrian-Refugees-and-Turkeys-Challenges-May-14–2014.pdf).

Kırmızıtaş, Hasan, Reşit Çelebioğlu, and Eyyüp Burun. 2016. "Kilis'te korku ve panik var, halkın yüzde 30'u göç etti. [30% of Kilis Population Left Due to Panic]." *CNN Turk*, April 26. Retrieved February 21, 2017 (www.cnnturk.com/turkiye/kiliste-korku-ve-panik-var-halkin-yuzde-30u-goc-etti).

Lenner, Katharina and Susanne Schmelter. 2016. "Syrian Refugees in Jordan and Lebanon: Between Refuge and Ongoing Deprivation?" *European Institute of the Mediterranean*. Retrieved February 21, 2017 (www.iemed.org/observatori/arees-danalisi/arxius-adjunts/anuari/med.2016/IEMed_MedYearBook2016_Refugges%20Jordan%20Lebanon_Lenner_Schmelter.pdf).

Lipset, Seymour Martin. 1959. "Some Social Requisites of Democracy: Economic Development and Political Legitimacy." *American Political Science Review* 53:69–105.

Martin, Michelle and Andrea Shalal. 2016. "Merkel: We Need Migrant Deals with African States Like EU-Turkey Pact." *Reuters*, September 16. (http://af.reuters.com/article/topNews/idAFKCN11W203).

McDonald-Gibson, Charlotte. 2016. "Refugee Crisis: Human Traffickers Netted Up to 4bn Last Year." *The Independent*. Retrieved February 21, 2017 (www.independent.co.uk/news/world/europe/refugee-crisis-human-traffickers-netted-up-to-4bn-last-year-a6816861.html).

Migration Policy Center. 2016. "The Syrian Refugee Crisis and Its Implications for the EU." Retrieved February 21, 2017 (http://syrianrefugees.eu/).

Ministry of Planning and International Cooperation, Jordan. 2014. "National Resilience Plan: 2014–2016." *Embassy of Jordan to the United States*, May 29. Retrieved February 21, 2017 (www.jordanembassyus.org/sites/default/files/NRP_FinalDraft_08.29.2014_MOPIC.pdf).

Organization for Economic Cooperation and Development. 2016a. "OECD Economic Survey of Turkey 2016." Retrieved February 21, 2017 (www.oecd.org/turkey/economic-survey-turkey.htm).

Organization for Economic Cooperation and Development. 2016b. "Turkey." Retrieved February 21, 2017 (https://data.oecd.org/turkey.htm).

ORSAM, Center for Middle Eastern Strategic Studies. 2015. "Effects of the Syrian Refugees on Turkey" (January). Report 195. Retrieved February 21, 2017 (www.orsam.org.tr/files/Raporlar/rapor195/195eng.pdf).

Poushter, Jacob. 2016. "European Opinions of the Refugee Crisis in 5 Charts." *Pew Research Center Fact Tank*. Retrieved February 21, 2017 (www.pewresearch.org/fact-tank/2016/09/16/european-opinions-of-the-refugee-crisis-in-5-charts/).

Przeworski, Adam, Michael E. Alvarez, José Antonio Cheibub, and Fernando Limongi. 2000. *Democracy and Development*. New York: Cambridge University Press.

Saliba, Issam. 2016. "Refugee Law and Policy: Lebanon." *Library of Congress*, March. Retrieved February 21, 2017 (www.loc.gov/law/help/refugee-law/lebanon.php?loclr=bloglaw).

Schimmelfennig, Frank, Stefan Engert, and Heiko Knobel. 2003. "Costs, Commitment and Compliance: The Impact of EU Democratic Conditionality on Latvia, Slovakia and Turkey." *Journal of Comparative Migration Studies* 41(3):495–518.

Sonmez, Mustafa. 2016. "Will Turkey's Negative Growth Rates Lead to Political Crisis?" *Al Monitor*. Retrieved February 21, 2017 (www.al-monitor.com/pulse/originals/2016/11/turkey-economy-in-harsh-fall-season.html).

UNHCR. 1951/2010. "Convention and Protocol Relating to the Status of Refugees." Retrieved February 21, 2017 (www.unhcr.org/en-us/3b66c2aa10).

UNHCR. 2016a. "3RP Education: Turkey Monthly Update-December." December 31. Retrieved February 19, 2017 (http://reliefweb.int/report/turkey/turkey-3rp-monthly-update-december-2016-education).

UNHCR. 2016b. "Legal Considerations on the Return of Asylum-Seekers and Refugees from Greece to Turkey as Part of the EU-Turkey Cooperation in Tackling the

Migration Crisis under the Safe Third Country and First Country of Asylum Concept." March 23. Retrieved February 21, 2017 (www.unhcr.org/56f3ec5a9.pdf).
UNHCR. 2016c. "UNHCR Map: Europe: Syrian Asylum Applications." Retrieved February 21, 2017 (http://data.unhcr.org/syrianrefugees/asylum.php).
UNHCR. 2017. "3RP Regional Refugee & Resilience Plan 2017–2018 in Response to the Syria Crisis." December 5. Retrieved February 19, 2017 (http://reliefweb.int/report/syrian-arab-republic/3rp-regional-refugee-resilience-plan-2017-2018-response-syria-crisis).
Winter, Chase. 2016. "Turkey Threatens to Cancel EU Migration Deal." *Deutsche Welle*. (www.dw.com/en/turkey-threatens-to-cancel-eu-migration-deal/a-36243636).
World Bank. 2015. *Turkey Data*. Retrieved February 21, 2017 (www.worldbank.org/en/country/turkey).
Yıldız, Ayselin and Elif Uzgören. 2016. "Limits to Temporary Protection: Non-Camp Syrian Refugees in Izmir, Turkey." *Southeast European and Black Sea Studies* 16(2):195–211.

4

THE EX-YUGOSLAV STATES AND THE 2015 REFUGEE/MIGRANT CRISIS

Victims or Opportunists?

Filip Kovačević

UNIVERSITY OF MONTENEGRO

> *Political and Military Sociology: An Annual Review*, 2017, Vol. 45: 54–70.
>
> Kelly Greenhill's book Weapons of Mass Migration: Forced Displacement, Coercion, and Foreign Policy, *the recipient of the 2011 International Studies Association's Book of the Year award, initiated a systematic study of the way state and non-state actors can and do engineer refugee/migrant crises to exert pressure on, and exact concessions from, the states they target. Greenhill identified three types of actors that may benefit from engineered migration flows: generators, agent provocateurs, and opportunists. In this article, I investigate to what extent, if at all, the ex-Yugoslav states that found themselves in the midst of the 2015 refugee/migrant crisis—the crisis which they neither generated nor actively provoked—were able to derive political rewards or payoffs from it. The ex-Yugoslav states included in my analysis are the Former Yugoslav Republic of Macedonia (FYROM), Serbia, Croatia, and Slovenia. In collecting the evidence and developing my thesis, I focus on refugee/migrant movements as reported chronologically in the local media and the public statements regarding the crisis by ex-Yugoslav states' political leaders.*

The subject of human migration has been studied in depth by a variety of disciplines in the past five decades. There are dozens of academic studies that approach migration from historical, anthropological, sociological, and juridical points of view. This article, however, has set itself a much more modest task. It is motivated by a single theoretical question which has important practical political implications: can migrant and refugee flows be "weaponized" by weaker states to pressure and blackmail the stronger, more politically powerful ones into making concessions? In her path-breaking 2010 book, *Weapons of Mass Migration*, Tufts University political science professor Kelly Greenhill argues that this indeed has been the case in the past. She also demonstrates that this kind of coercive, non-military strategy is not as infrequent and unsuccessful as is commonly thought.

However, there are immediate objections that can be put forward to formulating the question in this way. First, the question assumes that state elites behave as rational choice actors trying to maximize benefits (e.g., staying in power) while minimizing costs. The possession of perfect or near-perfect information is also assumed as to the conduct and results of planned activities. Third, the question neglects the role of other, non-state actors, such as non-governmental organizations and international agencies. And yet, Greenhill's careful and detailed empirical research on the period from 1951, when the U.N. Convention Relating to the Status of Refugees codified the rights of refugees and the obligations of states, to 2006 uncovers 56 *conclusive* attempts of what she calls "coercive engineered migration or migration-driven coercion."

Coercive engineered migrations are defined as "population movements that are deliberately created or manipulated in order to induce political, military and/or economic concessions from a target state or states" (Greenhill 2010b:13). Greenhill finds that, during the period under examination, coercive engineered migration occurred at the rate of about one case per year. This means that it was more frequent than interstate wars (0.68 cases per year) and intermediate deterrence crises (0.58 cases per year) (Greenhill 2010a:117). Moreover, she claims that it is possible that many other instances of successful coercion, threatened through secret state-to-state channels, went unreported or remain classified.

As to the successes of the coercive activities, Greenhill concludes that the generators of coercive engineered migration were fully successful in obtaining concessions from their targets in 57 percent of the cases, while they were at least partially successful in almost three-fourths of the cases (73 percent). For the sake of comparison, during the same time period, economic sanctions (typically used as the preferred weapon of non-military coercion) were effective in no more than 33 percent of the cases, while U.S. coercive diplomacy was successful only in 20–37 percent of the cases depending on how success is defined (Greenhill 2010a:121–2).

Greenhill shows that liberal democracies have been particularly vulnerable to the threats and practice of coercive engineered migration by their weaker, typically non-democratic opponents. This vulnerability derives from the internal functioning of a democratic system, which is grounded in two complementary types of liberalism: "normative or embedded liberalism," based on general norms and specific human rights legislation, and "political liberalism," based on the transparent and pluralist nature of political decision-making (Greenhill 2010a:136–7). The generators of coercive engineered migration are able to impose heavy "hypocrisy costs" on liberal democracies, defined by Greenhill as "symbolic political costs [stemming from the existence] of a real or perceived disparity between a professed commitment to liberal values and norms and demonstrated actions that contravene such a commitment" (Greenhill 2010b:4).

However, to complicate an already complicated strategic picture, in most cases of coercive engineered migration, including the one that is the subject of this article, there are even more interested parties or actors involved. In addition to the generator and the target(s), according to Greenhill, we can typically distinguish between *agents provocateurs* and opportunists. *Agents provocateurs* are those actors who "deliberately act in ways designed to incite others to generate outflows," while opportunists exploit the already generated outflows in order to derive political, economic, military, and security rewards or payoffs from them (Greenhill 2010a:119). For instance, in the case of the 1999 Kosovo refugee crisis, Greenhill indicates that the Kosovo Liberation Army (KLA) acted as the *agent provocateur* and the neighboring states of Albania and the Former Yugoslav Republic of Macedonia were opportunists (I would also add Montenegro to this category, though it was still within the Federal Republic of Yugoslavia at the time).

In this article, I intend to apply Greenhill's conceptual framework to the 2015 European refugee/migrant crisis. I plan to investigate to what extent the ex-Yugoslav states that found themselves in the midst of the crisis—a crisis which they neither generated nor actively provoked—were able to derive political benefits from it. The ex-Yugoslav states I will include in my analysis are the Former Yugoslav Republic of Macedonia (FYROM), Serbia, Croatia, and Slovenia. I will focus on refugee/migrant movements as reported chronologically by the local media during the summer and fall of 2015. I will also examine the public statements regarding the crisis by ex-Yugoslav states' political leaders directed primarily at their counterparts in the EU who were the primary targets of coercion.

Although the states under consideration were not long ago the constituent republics of one internationally recognized nation-state, the socialist Yugoslav federation, today they are very different. Slovenia is a fairly stable liberal democracy, whereas FYROM has faced many challenges on the road to political stability and democratic legitimacy. In addition, their institutional relations with the EU are also very different. Slovenia is a member of both the EU and the Schengen Zone. Croatia is a member of the EU, but not of the Schengen Zone. Serbia and FYROM are states-candidates for EU membership, but their membership seems a long way off. This is important to keep in mind when examining the strategies of their political elites.

Moreover, it should also be kept in mind that post–World War II Europe is no stranger to refugees/migrants from the Middle East and Africa.[1] From the late 1990s onwards, hundreds of thousands of individuals used the Mediterranean routes to Spain, Italy, and Greece in order to enter the European Union illegally. This trend intensified after the collapse of several autocratic regimes in the wake of the so-called Arab Spring in 2011. After the destruction of the Gaddafi regime in Libya and the start of civil war in Syria, the number of people leaving for Europe skyrocketed. Statistics compiled by the Pew Research Center show that in 2014, the EU (plus non-members Norway and Switzerland) received less than 700,000 asylum applications; in the following year, the number of applications increased to 1,325,000 (Connor 2016). Close to half of all the refugees/migrants who entered the EU in 2015 were from three countries of origin: Syria, Afghanistan, and Iraq. The vast majority entered via the so-called Balkan route, which involved crossing the borders of several ex-Yugoslav states. All had to pass through FYROM and Serbia, while Croatia and Slovenia were affected only when Hungary closed its borders, which happened fairly early in the crisis.

A Note on Methodology

For the purposes of this article, in order to gauge the reactions and discern the strategies of the ex-Yugoslav political elites concerning the unprecedented migrant/refugee crisis, it was necessary to collect the local media reports in chronological order. I opted for the Serb-Croat language wire services, such as TANJUG, BETA, and HINA, which provided almost daily coverage of the refugee/migrant issues from the beginning of the crisis. These reports were short, factual, and without any value judgments. I found the websites of the Serbian newspaper *Blic* and the Montenegrin newspaper *Vijesti* as the useful congregators of the wire service reports. I have also relied on the reports by the Balkan Investigative Reporting Network (BIRN), which brings together a group of independent media organizations from most ex-Yugoslav states, as well as on the reports by Al Jazeera Balkan, Radio Slobodna Evropa [Radio Free Europe], Reuters, and Deutsche Welle.

In terms of the period of coverage, I examined the entire duration of the crisis as it passed through the ex-Yugoslav states—that is, from June 2015 until January 2016—and reported on major developments, regardless of whether or not they fitted my theoretical framework. I also took care to briefly explain the political dynamic in each of the countries under consideration but focused on the local conditions only to the extent that they directly impacted the refugee/migrant issues. No doubt many nuances and flavors of the local political scenes have been lost in this way, but I think that the overall picture that emerges, which allows comparison among the different elites' political strategies and their arsenal of political skills and competencies, justifies this approach.

The First Ex-Yugoslav State on the Balkan Route: The Former Yugoslav Republic of Macedonia

In the spring of 2015, FYROM was going through a political crisis. Already divided along many lines, it at this time faced a public and violent confrontation between the ruling party, VMRO-DPMNE, led by long-time prime minister Nikola Gruevski, and the main opposition party, the Social Democratic Union of Macedonia (SDSM), led by Zoran Zaev. The opposition boycotted Parliament and organized frequent street demonstrations in the capital of Skopje. The antagonism was further deepened by the opposition's public release of the intercepted phone conversations between Gruevski and various top officials allegedly engaged in covering up a whole range of criminal activities.[2] In early May 2015, the western town of Kumanovo, already one of the main boiling points of violence during the 2001 Albanian-Macedonian conflict, was briefly attacked by a group of radical Albanian extremists. The Macedonian police swiftly intervened and either arrested or killed the extremists, but lost eight officers in the firefight. The background of the attack was never fully clarified and some observers underscored the direct political benefits that the scandal-ridden and badly shaken Gruevski government derived from this diversion of public attention (Reuters 2015). Be that as it may, it was precisely during this period of the extremely unstable, even explosive internal political situation in FYROM that the mass media began reporting the unprecedented increase in the refugee/migrant flow from Greece.

At that time, in late May and early June 2015, during the period which we can refer to as the initial stage of the 2015 refugee/migrant crisis, it was still believed that the Macedonian institutions might be able to deal with the influx on their own. In fact, news reports portrayed the Macedonian police as taking confident and decisive actions against what were called "illegal immigrants," and not refugees or migrants, as the case would be later on. For instance, one of the reports, published on June 11, 2015, described the arrest of 120 "illegal immigrants" from Syria and Iraq (Al-Jazeera Balkans 2015a). Obviously, this was thought to be "business as usual."

Soon enough, however, things began to change radically. The first inkling of that was the announcement that the Skopje government was changing the law on asylum. The changes allowed refugees/migrants to spend 72 hours in the country legally, during which time they would either have to apply for asylum or leave the country (Blic 2015a). Another provision allowed free use of public transport, which enabled faster transit through the country. Before that, the refugees/migrants typically transited by foot, following train tracks, which had led to the deaths of almost 30 individuals since the beginning of 2015. In some cases, they also bought bicycles from the local population at extremely inflated prices (Tanjug 2015a). In these instances, individual Macedonian citizens behaved opportunistically and derived economic benefits from the refugee/migrant flow. However, a key question of this article is to ascertain whether a variant of the same strategy was followed on the collective level as well. In other words, did the Macedonian ruling elites use their handling of the crisis to put pressure on and to sway the judgment of their international interlocutors, especially EU officials, in their favor?

The announcement of changes in the asylum law was followed by the statement of the Macedonian Minister of Interior Mitko Čavkov, who said that the number of "illegal immigrants" in FYROM had tripled compared to the same period in 2014 and that the trend was likely to continue (Tanjug 2015b). He also pointed out that immigrant reception camps and facilities were strained to the maximum (the same was stated in more dramatic terms by the Macedonian Ombudsman Idžet Memeti several days earlier) and that the ministry had already spent seven million Macedonian denars (U.S. $150,000) on their upkeep since the beginning of the year (BETA 2015b).

Čavkov's statement demonstrates the depth and difficulty of the crisis facing FYROM and the intensive efforts on the part of the Gruevski government to deal with it the best it could, but there was no explicit request for the involvement and assistance of the EU. The government still did not perceive the crisis as a potential bargaining chip.

Less than a month later, Skopje was visited by Victoria Nuland, U.S. Assistant Secretary of State for European and Eurasian affairs. Nuland met with the leadership of both the government and the opposition and pressured them to resolve the year-long political paralysis of the country. After the meetings, Nuland announced that she believed that a comprehensive agreement was near at hand (Al-Jazeera Balkans 2015b). This turned out to be correct. Just a day later, on July 14, 2015, the government and the opposition signed the so-called Pržino agreement that envisioned changes in the top government positions in favor of the opposition and early parliamentary elections in April 2016 (Independent 2015). For its part, the opposition agreed to return to Parliament and cease street protests. It should be noted that the agreement was signed in the presence of Johannes Hahn, the EU Commissioner for European Neighborhood Policy and Enlargement Negotiations, which gave it an international seal of approval.

However, the Pržino agreement fell apart in the coming months, and evidence suggests that the Gruevski government began using the refugee/migrant crisis opportunistically in order to get Brussels to support its political agenda. Initially, the government treated the refugees/migrants with strong-arm police tactics, including humiliations, arrests, and even beatings. The British press, for instance, reported in early July 2015 that the Macedonian police severely abused several young Syrian refugees at the Greek-Macedonian border (BETA 2015c). This "bad image" was cemented by a harshly critical report of Amnesty International (BETA 2015d). At the same time, the government's public appeals to the EU and other international organizations were minimal. These policies were in stark contrast with those pursued by the government of Serbia under Aleksandar Vučić.

It appears, however, that after the Pržino agreement, Gruevski (and the president of FYROM Gjorge Ivanov) realized the profitability of what Vučić had been doing all along and began to seek close cooperation—meaning an infusion of funds—and coordination with the EU. For instance, in the first announcement of its kind, on July 17, 2015, it was reported that the Macedonian government was willing to close its borders in coordination with other EU and non-EU countries on the Balkan refugee/migrant route, especially the countries of the Višegrad group (Hungary, the Czech Republic, Slovakia, and Poland) (SRNA 2015).

However, at that time, the EU member states did not feel enough political pressure to take this offer seriously. What Greenhill calls "hypocrisy costs" were still too low for the EU to engage with Macedonia. For instance, Jean Asselborn, the foreign minister of Luxembourg, who took over the presidency of the Council of the European Union in the summer of 2015, stated in August 2015 that the EU would accept no more than 60,000 refugees/migrants by the end of the year (Kuzmanovski 2015). This was probably one of the most short-sighted statements in the history of European diplomacy. While the Macedonian-Greek border did indeed close, it was not until more than six months later. By this time, more than one million refugees/migrants had already crossed into Western Europe.

The Second Ex-Yugoslav State on the Balkan Route: Serbia

Already in the last weeks of June 2015, the Serbian mass media reported that more than a thousand refugees/migrants were crossing the Serbian-Macedonian border every day. Most of them were directed to the Preševo region of southern Serbia, which has a majority Albanian population and was the center of a violent anti-government insurgency in 1999–2001. Whether there was a cynical intent behind this decision by the Serbian authorities is difficult to say. In this respect, one should recall, for instance, how the Serbian refugees from the Krajina region of Croatia were re-settled in Kosovo after being violently expelled by the Croatian military in 1995. Be that as it may, Preševo soon turned into "a town of refugees" (Tanjug 2015c). The top Serbian government officials began to visit it frequently and the government authorized the construction of large scale facilities to house refugees/migrants.

And yet, the July report of Amnesty International, cited above, condemned Serbia for its treatment of refugees/migrants just as harshly as it condemned FYROM. In contrast to the Macedonian government, the government in Belgrade reacted immediately. The very next day, Aleksandar Vulin, the minister of social affairs, rejected the report's claims and stated that not a single "migrant" was mistreated by the Serbian police or by anybody else in Serbia. He denied that the police or "any other [state] formation" extorted money from the "migrants" (Tanjug 2015d).

On July 15, 2015, during a visit to Preševo, Prime Minister Vučić delivered what can be considered the key statement regarding his government's approach (Tanjug 2015e). He asserted that Serbia would pool all its resources to enable the smooth and dignified transit of the refugees/migrants through its territory. At the same time, he stressed that the Serbian state was spending in the excess of €15,000 every day and that the state budget would soon not be able to bear further costs without EU assistance. Vučić claimed that the existing EU migrant/refugee policy was not "responsible enough." He called on the EU to craft a joint policy approach with the transit countries and enforce it in full.

By taking this approach, Vučić put the pressure not on the refugees/migrants—as the Macedonian government had done—but on EU officials and institutions. He intended to ratchet up the "hypocrisy costs" for the EU by emphasizing the gap between its liberal rhetoric of freedom of movement and human rights and the actual policies of EU governments. He positioned Serbia as a country that was ready and willing to honor "liberal European" values even though it was not a member of the EU. He intentionally amplified the theme that "Serbia is more European than Europe" in order to exploit it in the tough negotiations on Serbia's EU accession as well as in the EU-sponsored talks with the Kosovo Albanian leadership (Tanjug 2015e).

As subsequent events have shown, Vučić's strategy bore fruit as the EU leadership soon silenced internal opposition from certain member states, such as Croatia, and opened two accession chapters for Serbia (32 on financial control and 35 on other issues) in December 2015 and two (23 on judicial and fundamental rights and 24 on justice, freedom, and security) in July 2016 (B92 2016). The EU also began to be less inclined to support the demands of Kosovo Albanians regarding the position of the Serb minority and its institutional links with Serbia (Zejneli 2016).

Concurrently with the worsening of the refugee/migrant crisis on its southern border with Macedonia, Serbia was faced with what turned out to be a very serious issue with long-term political and economic repercussions on its northern border with Hungary, an EU and NATO member state. In June 2015, Hungarian Prime Minister Viktor Orban publicly stated that the government planned to submit a new law to the Hungarian Parliament which would effectively close the borders to the refugees/migrants whom he referred to as "illegal immigrants" (N.V. 2015). He also insisted that the EU-imposed quotas were "at the edge of reason" and that Hungary would not enforce them. Antal Rogan, the parliamentary head of Orban's political party Fidesz, claimed that "immediate measures" were needed because over 50,000 refugees/migrants entered Hungary by May 2015, whereas there were only 43,000 in all of 2014 (N.V. 2015).

The political tensions between Serbia and Hungary quickly escalated when it was announced in mid-June 2015 that Hungary was not only contemplating closing borders, but also building a 4-meter high fence, a type of physical barrier not seen in Europe since the days of the Communist bloc and the Berlin Wall. In less than 25 years, Hungary had gone from a country that had border fences to keep people in to one that built them to keep people out.

The Serbian government's reaction was swift. It announced a meeting with its Hungarian counterparts for July 1, 2015, and unofficially called the decision "unjust." The Serbian minister of the Interior Nebojša Stefanović called on the EU to do a better job in protecting its external borders with Greece and Bulgaria and stated that Serbia was doing more than its share "even though it is not in the EU" (Jelovac 2015). The July meeting between Vučić and Orban brought no relief for the Serbian side, however (Vasiljević 2015). Orban was determined to build the fence, and he had the support of the Parliament and a sizeable portion of the public. Already in August 2015, there was a sense that the closing of the Hungarian border was imminent. This precipitated a significant increase in the number of refugees/migrants transiting Serbia (Blic 2015b). The Serbian government then quietly began bussing refugees/migrants to the border with Croatia.

The Third Ex-Yugoslav State on the Balkan Route: Croatia

The preferred destination of the vast majority of refugees/migrants was Germany. The shortest Balkan route to Germany led from the Former Yugoslav Republic of Macedonia via Serbia and Hungary and, by August 2015, almost all refugees/migrants traveled that route. However, as Hungary began to construct the fence on its border with Serbia, the route shifted to Croatia and the Croatian-Hungarian border. The first organized group of refugees/migrants, about 500 of them, entered the Croatian town of Tovarnik from Serbia on September 16, 2015 (Slobodna Dalmacija 2015). The Croatian government immediately formed a special government body for the coordination of all refugee/migrant issues headed by the Deputy Prime Minister and Interior Minister Ranko Ostojić.

Ostojić soon became the main protagonist of bitter disputes with top Serbian officials over the direction of migrant/refugee flows. On September 17, 2015, just one day after a large group of refugees/migrants entered Croatia, Ostojić stated that Croatia could "accept no more people," implying that Serbia should stop bussing them to the border (Zebić 2015). Hostilities over the same issue also flared up between Prime Minister Vučić and the Croatian Prime Minister Zoran Milanović (Deutsche Welle 2015). At times, these exchanges sank to the level of infantilistic banality. At one point, for instance, referring to the Serbian warning that it would seek redress at the international tribunals in charge of safeguarding human rights if Croatia closed its borders and returned refugees/migrants to Serbia, Milanović stated that "we are an eagle. And an eagle does not hunt flies." The Serbian foreign minister Ivica Dačić responded with a line from the cult Yugoslav 1980s spy movie, *The Balkan Spy*: "The eagle fell" (HINA 2015b).

However, as the number of refugees/migrants from Serbia increased exponentially in the second part of September, some observers expressed concern that the two states might resort to violence. The war of words escalated and Croatia even briefly closed most of its border crossings with Serbia (B-92/Index.hr 2015). Milanović made headlines by stating that Hungary was building the fence on the Hungarian-Serbian border because it considered the Serbs "barbarians."[3]

The severity of the problem between the two states stemmed, in large part, from the fact that the initial directives Croatia received from the EU were not only general and vague, but also to a great extent unrealistic. Considering that Croatia is not a member of the Schengen Zone, the Brussels bureaucrats demanded that it register and keep all the refugees/migrants on its territory. This was far from feasible because the refugee/migrant inflow from Serbia numbered in the thousands and sometimes involved more than 10,000 individuals a day (HINA/HRT 2015c).

In addition, Croatian parliamentary elections were scheduled for November 2015. Due to the lingering sense of economic crisis, including rising unemployment among the younger population (HINA/HRT 2015d), Croatian voters were increasingly turning away from the ruling coalition headed by Milanović's Social Democrats in favor of the conservative opposition led by Tomislav Karamarko's Croatian Democratic Community (HDZ).

Considering this turn of events, exacting concessions or trying to blackmail the EU by using the refugee/migrant influx opportunistically was far from Milanović's list of priorities. Instead, his key electoral strategy was to project a hardline attitude toward Croatia's ex-Yugoslav neighbors. In July 2015, Milanović decided to withdraw unilaterally from the arbitration of a long-running border dispute with Slovenia before the Permanent Court of Arbitration located in The Hague (HRT 2015). He amplified his nationalist rhetoric against Serbia, hoping it would distract voters.

This electoral strategy failed and Milanović lost the elections held on November 11, 2015. In January 2016, a new ruling coalition was formed between the conservative HDZ and the independent political grouping, "The Bridge" (Most), with the non-partisan ex-businessman Tihomir Orešković, a Croatian-Canadian, becoming prime minister (HINA/HRT 2016). However, by this time, the refugee/migrant crisis had greatly subsided and the potential for using it as a bargaining chip with the Brussels bureaucracy had disappeared.

It should be noted that the overall EU policy guidelines to Croatia were inadequate in another sense as well. There was no way to stop the refugees/migrants in Croatia because they wanted to leave the country as soon as they entered it. In a dramatically urgent manner, they pressed on toward Croatia's northern borders with Hungary and Slovenia. Already in late September and early October 2015, Orban ordered the fence, already placed on the Hungarian-Serbian border, to be extended to cover the Hungarian-Croatian border as well (HINA 2015a). This made Slovenia and its border with Austria the only option for migrants/refugees attempting to get to Germany as quickly as possible. Thus Slovenia became the fourth and last ex-Yugoslav state to find itself on the 2015 Balkan refugee/migrant route.

The Fourth Ex-Yugoslav State on the Balkan Route: Slovenia

Much like FYROM at the beginning of the crisis, Slovenia initially tried to keep the refugees/migrants out by force. There were news reports that Slovenian border guards used tear gas against refugees/migrants, including women and children, and the Slovenian Parliament authorized the military to assist the police in keeping law and order in the border areas (Tanjug 2015f). Clearly, the entire governmental structure was in severe crisis mode. However, unlike what happened in FYROM, the Slovenian leadership, headed by Prime Minister Miro Cerar and President Borut Pahor, immediately put intense pressure on the EU bureaucracy to help Slovenia financially and logistically. Mere days after thousands of refugees/migrants began arriving in Slovenia, Cerar announced that the EU's assistance was already making a difference in the Slovene ability to deal with the crisis (Tanjug 2015g). Slovenian politicians repeatedly stressed that Slovenia was "the smallest" country on the Balkan refugee/migrant route and that therefore it required the most assistance from the EU. Slovenia was also the most prosperous among the countries in question, but this fact was, for obvious reasons, conveniently dropped out of the official narrative.

The success of the Slovenian government vis-à-vis the EU was particularly irksome to its counterpart in Croatia and, for this reason, the two governments constantly accused each other of bad faith (Tanjug 2015h). There was a sense among the members of the Milanović government that the EU did not pay enough attention to the Croatian troubles, but there was also no coherent strategy as to how to play the migrant/refugee card in the best possible way to gain political advantage. After Milanović was defeated at the polls, but before the new government was formed, the relations between Slovenia and Croatia deteriorated further (BETA 2015a).

Slovenia also successfully resisted the initiative of the Austrian and German governments to set up joint Slovenian-Austrian-German border controls on the Slovenian border with Croatia, the border of the Schengen Zone. As the Interior Minister Vesna Gjerkeš Žnidar pointed out, this put Slovenia in danger of becoming a "permanent" refugee zone for those whom Austria and Germany did not want (BETA 2016). She demanded that all refugees/migrants be registered in Croatia, considering that Croatia, and not Slovenia, was the first EU country they entered from Serbia.

The Waning of the 2015 Refugee/Migrant Crisis

As 2015 came to an end, and with over a million refugees/migrants having entered the EU, it was clear that a more comprehensive and long-term strategy would have to be created and directed toward those who generated the crisis. This meant offering a great deal of concessions to Turkey, where most of the refugees/migrants were based before their trek to the West. The negotiations between the EU and Turkey began in early 2016 and were concluded on March 18 (European Commission 2016). The EU promised to give Turkey €3 billion immediately and another 3 billion by the end of 2018 to liberalize the EU visa travel regime for Turkish citizens and to put new vigor into the negotiations on Turkey's accession to the EU. For its part, Turkey agreed to stop any migrants/refugees from leaving its territory and to take back all Syrian migrants/refugees who landed on any Greek island after March 20, 2016. Regarding the latter, the EU promised to re-settle in the EU one Syrian refugee sent directly from Turkey for every Syrian refugee that Turkey took back from Greece.

Using Greenhill's conceptual framework, one can conclude that Turkey profited greatly from its role as the stepping-off point to Europe, as the EU was forced to make both financial and institutional concessions. As soon as the benefits of the concessions started trickling in, the flow of refugees was reduced greatly. More than anything else, this exposed the strategic aspect of the crisis. From hundreds of thousands, the numbers were down to several hundred in just a few days. The power of the Turkish state "suddenly" started making itself felt in its border regions.

Hand in hand with the EU-Turkey deal, the government of FYROM, in cooperation primarily with the governments of Austria and the Višegrad group, decided to close its border with Greece. Already in February 2016, the authorities in Skopje were letting in only refugees/migrants from Syria and returning all others to Greece. In March 2016, the ban became total (Bucalo 2016). This led to the humanitarian catastrophe at the Idomeni refugee/migrant camp right across the border in Greece. More than 20,000 people, including many children, found themselves in disastrous living conditions. Their pain and suffering caused an international outcry, but it took more than two months for the Greek government to evacuate the camp (Kitsantonis 2016).

The Macedonian Foreign Minister Nikola Poposki justified the border closure by claiming that FYROM wanted to be a part of the EU (Deutsche Welle 2016). Throughout 2016, the government of Macedonia used its activities directed against the illegal border crossings to pressure the EU into speeding up accession negotiations. Thus, in contrast to the initial phases of the crisis, the Macedonian government used its waning phase in an opportunistic manner.

Concluding Remarks

The innovative application of the conceptual framework elaborated by Kelly Greenhill has provided yet another way to understand and evaluate the important political strategies of the ex-Yugoslav states—the Former Yugoslav Republic of Macedonia, Serbia, Croatia, and Slovenia—that found themselves in the midst of the 2015 refugee/migrant crisis. It is of course far from being the only possible way of interpreting these strategies, but it has provided several useful insights.

First of all, the application of this framework reveals that not every government had equal levels of skill and success in using the crisis as a bargaining chip to achieve its own foreign policy goals vis-à-vis the target states of the EU. Not all profited politically from the crisis in equal measure, and one—the government of Croatia—may have even lost its hold on power in part due to its inadequate handling of the refugee/migrant inflows.

By contrast, the government of Serbia was able to derive the most concessions and benefits from the EU on account of its opportunistic use of the crisis. From the very beginning, the Serbian prime minister branded the crisis as an EU problem *par excellence* and demanded that the EU be heavily involved both financially and logistically. The EU quickly conceded to Vučić's demands, and Vučić's position regarding the Kosovo negotiations also improved. In fact, there is a stark contrast between the way that EU members Croatia, Slovenia, and Hungary handled the crisis and the way it was handled by Serbia. One can say that Serbia demonstrated a much more serious commitment to so-called European values than any of the other three ex-Yugoslav states.

Another government that was able to navigate the crisis fairly successfully, while pushing its own national interests forward, was the Slovenian government. As in the case of Serbia, the Slovenes demanded the assistance and accountability of the EU, and they got what they wanted for the most part. Their attitude and behavior toward the refugees/migrants was more heavy-handed than Serbia's, but less brutal than FYROM's.

In fact, it appears that the Macedonian government was the least prepared to deal with the consequences of the crisis and exploit it successfully. This can be explained by the fact that FYROM was the first ex-Yugoslav state to confront the refugee/migrant flow and had no previous experience in dealing with a crisis of this magnitude. In the first weeks of the crisis, for instance, the Macedonian government acted as if it could deal with the refugee/migrant influx on its own, using only repressive measures. This clearly turned out to be not only short-sighted, but it also exposed the country to devastating international criticism. However, as I have already indicated, the government learned from its mistakes and, by the end of the summer, obtained concessions from the EU. In fact, one can argue that the prime minister was able to prolong his stay in power for another several months precisely because he positioned himself as the key EU (and the Višegrad group) partner.

The biggest victim of the crisis was the government of Zoran Milanović in Croatia. Not only did that government's nationalistic behavior toward the neighboring states of Serbia and Slovenia raise the ugly specter of a new violent Balkan conflict and earn the reproof of the EU bureaucracy, but it also failed to win the confidence of voters and lost the November 2015 parliamentary elections. While its problematic handling of the crisis was not the sole reason it lost those elections (the dismal unemployment picture seems to have been more important), there is no doubt that the way Milanović handled the crisis did not translate into political gain. The new government of the non-partisan ex-businessman Tihomir Orešković turned out to be much more of a team player in the region and was praised by neighboring states. However, it also had an easier job than its predecessor because, when it was formed at the end of January 2016, the refugee/migrant crisis was already about to be contained by the EU-Turkey agreement.

However, for unrelated, internal political reasons, this government was short-lived, and the new parliamentary elections in Croatia, held in September 2016, led to a center-right dominated Parliament and the conservative-led government of Prime Minister Andrej Plenković. To what extent these ideological changes will make the intra-regional cooperation smoother should another refugee/migrant crisis sweep over the Balkans remains to be seen.

Overall, it can be said that the 2015 refugee/migrant crisis revealed serious weaknesses in the institutional frameworks of all ex-Yugoslav states. While conventional thinking assumes that the crisis was more damaging in the states that were further away institutionally from the EU, the application of Greenhill's theoretical framework makes evident that this has not been the case. Instead, whether the crisis brought political losses or profits depended on the skills of a given state's elites. Political leadership, not simply the blind force of circumstances, made a big difference.

Notes

1 Considering that there has been a great deal of acrimonious debate over the use of different terms to describe those taking part in mass migrations to Europe, I use the term "refugee/migrant" in order to maintain academic neutrality. The legal status of these individuals is not relevant for the thesis of the chapter (see Ruz 2015).
2 See, for instance, Marusic (2015a, 2015b).
3 That segment of the press conference can be watched here: www.youtube.com/watch?v=-vSoniR2uuQ.

References

Al-Jazeera Balkans. 2015a. "Uhapšeno 120 Illegalnih Imigranata. [120 Illegal Immigrants Arrested]." *Al-Jazeera Balkans*, June 11. Retrieved February 21, 2017 (http://balkans.aljazeera.net/vijesti/makedonija-uhapseno-120ilegalnih-imigranata).

Al-Jazeera Balkans. 2015b. "Nuland: Vrijeme da Makedonija Krene Naprijed. [Nuland: It's Time for Macedonia to Go Forward]." *Al-Jazeera Balkans*, July 13. Retrieved February 21, 2017 (http://balkans.aljazeera.net/vijesti/nuland-vrijeme-da-makedonijakrene-naprijed).

B92. 2016. "Sutra Otvaranje Poglavlja 23 i 24: Srbija u E.U. do 2025? [Tomorrow the Opening of Chapters 23 and 24: Serbia in the EU until 2025?" *B92*, July 17. Retrieved February 21, 2017 (www.b92.net/info/vesti/index.php?yyyy=2016&mm=07&dd=17&nav_id=1156157).

B-92/Index.hr. 2015. "Hrvatska Zatvorila Sve Granice Prema Srbiji. [Croatia Closed All Borders with Serbia]." *B92*, September 17. Retrieved February 21, 2017 (www.b92.net/info/vesti/index.php?yyyy=2015&mm=09&dd=17&nav_id=1040763).

BETA. 2015a. "Žičana Ograda ne Prejudicira Granicu. [The Wire Fence Does Not Predetermine the Border]." *BETA*, November 13. Retrieved February 21, 2017 (www.vijesti.me/specijali/zicana-ograda-ne-prejudicira-granicu-860453).

BETA. 2015b. "Ombudsman Kritikovao Vladu Makedonije Zbog Odnosa Prema Imigrantima. [Ombudsman Criticized Macedonian Government Because of Its Attitude toward Immigrants]." *BETA*, June 12. Retrieved February 21, 2017 (http://beta.rs/vesti/126-drustvo-vesti-region/5773ombudsman-kritikovao-vladu-makedonijezbog-odnosa-prema-imigrantima).

BETA. 2015c. "Oštre Optužbe—Britanski Mediji: Makedonski Policajci Tuku Migrante Na Granici. [Sharp Accusations: The British Media: Macedonia Police Officers Beat Migrants at the Border]." *BETA*, July 11. Retrieved February 21, 2017 (www.blic.rs/vesti/svet/ostre-optuzbebritanski-mediji-makedonski-policajci-tuku-migrante-na-granici/wm71eps).

BETA. 2015d. "Amnesti: Srbija i Makedonija Ponor za Izbeglice Koje Evropska Unija Neće. [Amnesty International: Serbia and Macedonia Abyss for Refugees Not Wanted by the European Union]." *BETA*, July 7. Retrieved February 21, 2017 (www.blic.rs/vesti/drustvo/amnesti-srbija-imakedonija-ponor-za-izbeglice-koje-evropska-unija-nece/etxjl43).

BETA. 2016. "Slovenija Odbila Zajedničku Kontrolu Granice. [Slovenia Refused Joint Control of Borders]." *BETA*, January 18. Retrieved February 21, 2017 (www.vijesti.me/specijali/slovenija-odbila-zajednicku-kontrolu-granice870681).

Blic. 2015a. "Makedonska Vlada Menja Zakon O Azilu. [Macedonian Government Changes Law on Asylum]." *Blic*, June 17. Retrieved February 21, 2017 (www.blic.rs/vesti/svet/makedonija-menja-zakon-o-azilu/7815rzy).

Blic. 2015b. "Reke Migranata: Vozovi Na Đevđeliji Puni Ljudi Koji Nadiru Prema Srbiji. Rivers of Migrants: Trains from Gevgeliya Packed with People Coming to Serbia]." *Blic*, August 12. Retrieved February 21, 2017 (www.blic.rs/vesti/drustvo/reke-migranata-vozovi-nadjevdeliji-puni-ljudi-koji-nadiru-prema-srbiji/k406bdw).

Bucalo, Elvir. 2016. "Zatvorena 'Balkanska Ruta' Za Migrante. [The 'Balkan Route' Closed for Migrants]." *Glas Amerike [Voice of America]*, March 9. Retrieved February 21, 2017 (www.glasamerike.net/a/migrant-crisis-macedonia-close-border-eu-parliament-criticize-summit-in-turkey/3227776.html).

Connor, Philip. 2016. "Number of Refugees to Europe Surges to Record 1.3 Million in 2015." *Pew Research Center*, August 2. Retrieved February 21, 2017 (www.pewglobal.org/2016/08/02/number-of-refugees-to-europe-surges-to-record1-3-million-in-2015).

Deutsche Welle. 2015. "Izbjeglička Kriza Dodatno Posvađala Susjede. [Migrant Crisis Further Antagonized Neighbors]." *Deutsche Welle*, September 23. Retrieved February 21, 2017 (www.dw.com/hr/izbjeglička-kriza-dodatnoposvađala-susjede/a-18735049).

Deutsche Welle. 2016. "Makedonija Zatvorila Granice Jer Želi Biti Dio E.U. [Macedonia Closed Borders Because It Wants to Be a Member of the E.U.]." *Deutsche Welle*, October 21. Retrieved February 21, 2017 (www.dw.com/bs/makedonija-je-zatvorila-granice-jer%C5%BEeli-biti-dio-eu/a-36110531).

European Commission. 2016. "Implementing the E.U.-Turkey Statement." *EC Press Release Database*, June 15. Retrieved February 21, 2017 (http://europa.eu/rapid/press-release_MEMO-161664_en.htm).

Greenhill, Kelly M. 2010a. "Weapons of Mass Migration: Forced Displacement as an Instrument of Coercion." *Strategic Insights* 9(1):116–59.

Greenhill, Kelly M. 2010b. *Weapons of Mass Migration: Forced Displacement, Coercion, and Foreign Policy*. Ithaca, NY: Cornell University Press.

HINA. 2015a. "Orban: Ograda je Neuništiva, Izbjeglice je ne mogu Probiti.[Orban: The Fence Is Indestructible, Refuges Cannot Penetrate It]." *HINA*, October 25. Retrieved February 28, 2017 (www.vecernji.hr/svijet/orban-ograda-je-neunistiva-izbjeglicejene-mogu-probiti-1033080).

HINA. 2015b. "Milanović: Orao Ne Lovi Muhe, a Mi Smo Orao; Dačić: Orao Pao. [Milanović: Eagles Does Not Hunt Flies, and We are Eagle: Dačić: Eagle Down]." *HINA*, September 18. Retrieved February 21, 2017 (www.index.hr/vijesti/clanak/milanovic-orao-ne-lovimuhe-a-mi-smo-orao-dacic-orao-je-pao/842797.aspx).

HINA/HRT. 2015c. "Izbjeglice i Dalje Stižu u Hrvatsku Preko Srbije. [Refuges Still Arrive in Croatia Via Serbia]." *HINA/HRT*, October 2. Retrieved February 21, 2017 (www.tportal.hr/vijesti/hrvatska/398917/Izbjeglice-i-dalje-stizuu-Hrvatsku-preko-Srbije.html).

The Ex-Yugoslav States   69

HINA/HRT. 2015d. "Broj Nezaposlenih Opet Raste. [Number of Unemployed Again on the Increase]." *Index*, October 10. Retrieved February 21, 2017 (www.index.hr/vijesti/clanak/broj-nezaposlenih-opet-raste/847689.aspx).

HINA/HRT. 2016. "Ovo je Program Oreškovićeve Vlade. [This Is the Program of Orešković' Government]." *HINA/HRT*, January 22. Retrieved February 22, 2017 (www.hrt.hr/318534/vijesti/mandatar-oreskovic-u-saboru-predstavioprogramsvoje-vlade).

HRT. 2015. "Hrvatska Izlazi iz Arbitraže, Slovenija Izigrala Temelje. [Croatia Leaves Arbitration, Slovenia Betrayed the Principles]." *HRT*, July 27. Retrieved February 21, 2017 (http://vijesti.hrt.hr/293404/milanovic-i-celnici-stranaka-o-sudbini-arbitraznogs porazuma-sa-slovenijom).

Independent. 2015. "Przino Deal: What Did Leaders Sign?" *The Independent: The Macedonian English Language Agency*, July 15. Retrieved February 21, 2017 (www.independent.mk/articles/19769/Przino+Deal+What+Did+Leaders+Sign).

Jelovac, B. 2015. "Mađarski Zid: Pobesneli Orban Hoće da Podigne Ogradu Prema Srbiji. [The Hungarian Wall: Enraged Orban Wants to Build a Fence toward Serbia." *Blic*, June 18. Retrieved February 21, 2017 (www.blic.rs/vesti/politika/madjarski-zid-pobesneliorban-hoce-da-podigne-ogradu-prema-srbiji/vgqv2mc).

Kitsantonis, Niki. 2016. "Greece Begins Moving Refugees Out of Idomeni Camp." *New York Times*, May 24. Retrieved February 21, 2017 (www.nytimes.com/2016/05/25/world/europe/greece-idomeni-refugee-camp.html).

Kuzmanovski, Blagoja. 2015. "Makedonija: Hiljade Migranata Dnevno, Situacija Sve Gora. [Macedonia: Thousands of Migrants a Day, Situation Getting Worse]." *Radio Slobodna Evropa [Radio Free Europe]*, August 17. Retrieved February 21, 2017 (www.slobodnaevropa.org/a/makedonija-hiljade-migranata-dnevno-situacija-svegora/27193512.html).

Marusic, Sinisa Jakov. 2015a. "New Tapes Show Macedonia Prime Minister Fixing Cuts." *BIRN*, March 26. Retrieved March 13, 2017 (www.balkaninsight.com/en/article/tapes-macedonian-pm-entangled-in-large-scalecorruption).

Marusic, Sinisa Jakov. 2015b. "Macedonia Tapes Suggest Government Meddling with Lustration." *BIRN*, April 8. Retrieved March 13, 2017 (www.balkaninsight.com/en/article/tapes-reveal-political-meddling-withmacedonian-lustration).

N.V. 2015. "Stop Za Azilante: Orban Hoće Da Zatvori Granicu Mađarske Prema Srbiji. [Stop for Asylum Seekers: Orban Wants to Close the Hungarian-Serbia Border]." *Blic*, June 9. Retrieved February 21, 2017 (www.blic.rs/vesti/svet/stop-za-azilante-orban-hoceda-zatvori-granicu-madarske-prema-srbiji/4bkhfyl-madjarska).

Reuters. 2015. "Violence between Macedonia Police and 'Terrorists' Increases Scrutiny of Prime Minister [Gruevski]." *Reuters*, May 11. Retrieved February 21, 2017 (www.theguardian.com/world/2015/may/11/macedonia-violence-nikola-gruevskigovernment).

Ruz, Camila. 2015. "The Battle Over the Words Used to Describe Migrants." *BBC News Magazine*, August 28. Retrieved March 13, 2017 (www.bbc.com/news/magazine 34061097).

Slobodna Dalmacija. 2015. "Stigle Izbjeglice U Hrvatsku: Preko 500 Primljeno ih je U Tovarniku. [Refuges Arrived in Croatia: More Than 500 Received in Tovarnik]." *Slobodna Dalmacija*, September 16. Retrieved February 21, 2017 (www.slobodnadalmacija.hr/novosti/hrvatska/clanak/id/286466/stigle-izbjeglice-uhrvatsku-preko-500-primljeno-ih-je-u-tovarniku).

SRNA. 2015. "Makedonija Spremna Za Zatvaranje Granica Za Migrante [Macedonia Ready to Closer Borders for Migrants]." *SRNA*, July 17. Retrieved February 21, 2017 (www.blic.rs/vesti/drustvo/makedonija-spremna-za-zatvaranjegranica-za-migrante/khj72md).

Tanjug. 2015a. "Makedonski Trgovci se Bogate na Račun Migranata. [Macedonia Merchants Are Getting Rich Taking Advantage of Migrants]." *Tanjug*, June 11. Retrieved February 21, 2017 (www.blic.rs/vesti/svet/makedonski-trgovci-se-bogate-na-racunmigranata/l5dc06k).

Tanjug. 2015b. "Migranti će Imati Pravo na 72 Sata Legalnog Boravka u Makedoniji. [Migrants will have a Right to 72 Hours of Legal Residence in Macedonia]." *Tanjug*, June 18. Retrieved February 21, 2017 (www.blic.rs/vesti/svet/migranti-ce-imati-pravo-na-72-satalegalnog-boravka-u-makedoniji/5n1x3lr).

Tanjug. 2015c. "Granicu Između Srbije i Makedonije Dnevno Pređe Više Od 1.000 Migranata. [Border between Serbia and Macedonia Is Crossed by More Than 1,000 Migrants a Day]." *Tanjug*, June 24. Retrieved February 21, 2017 (www.blic.rs/vesti/drustvo/granicu-izmedusrbije-i-makedonije-dnevno-prede-vise-od-1000-migranata/zfrnv2b).

Tanjug. 2015d. "Vulin: Netačan Izvještaj Amnesti Internešenela. [Vulin: The Amnesty International Report Incorrect]." *Blic*, July 8. Retrieved February 21, 2017 (www.blic.rs/vesti/politika/vulin-netacan-izvetaj-amnestiinternesenela/lpxyhtf).

Tanjug. 2015e. "Vučić: Politika Eu Prema Migrantima Nedovoljno Odgovorna. [Vučić: EU Policy toward Migrants Not Responsible Enough]." *Blic*, July 15. Retrieved February 21, 2017 (www.blic.rs/vesti/politika/vucic-politika-eu-prema-migrantimane dovoljno-odgovorna/ds247rn).

Tanjug. 2015f. "Slovenija: Policija Suzavcem Na Izbjeglice. [Slovenia: Tear Gas against Migrants]." *Vijesti*, October 20. Retrieved February 21, 2017 (www.vijesti.me/specijali/slovenija-policija-suzavcem-na-izbjeglice-856590).

Tanjug. 2015g. "Cerar: Slovenija će Dobiti Evropsku Pomoć. [Cerar: Slovenia Will Get European Assistance]." *Vijesti*, October 21. Retrieved February 21, 2017 (www.vijesti.me/specijali/cerar-slovenija-ce-dobiti-evropsku-pomoc-856774).

Tanjug. 2015h. "Cerar: Saradnja Sa Austrijom Dobra, Sa Hrvatskom Ne. [Cerar: Cooperation with Austria is Good, with Croatia, Not Good]." *Vijesti*, October 21. Retrieved February 21, 2017 (www.vijesti.me/specijali/cerar-saradnja-s-austrijom-dobra-shrvatskom-ne-856822).

Vasiljević, Predrag. 2015. "Budimpešta: Zid Nije Protiv Srpskog Naroda; Beograd: Nije Prijatno. [Budapest: The Wall Is Not against the Serbian People: Belgrade: It Is Not Pleasant]." *Večernje Novosti*, July 1. Retrieved February 21, 2017 (www.novosti.rs/vesti/naslovna/politika/aktuelno.289.html:555444-BudimpestaZid-nije-protiv-srpskog-naroda-Beograd-Nije-prijatno).

Zebić, Enes. 2015. "Ministar Policije Ostojić: Hrvatska Ne Može Primati Više Ljudi. [Minister of Police Ostojić: Croatia Cannot Receive Any More People]." *Slobodna Dalmacija*, September 17. Retrieved February 21, 2017 (www.slobodnaevropa.org/a/preko-pethiljada-ljudi-uslo-u-hrvatsku/27253326.html).

Zejneli, Amra. 2016. "Zajednica Srpskih Opština Na Čekanju. [The Alliance of Serbian Municipalities Put on the Waiting List]." *Slobodna Evropa [Radio Free Europe]*, January 5. Retrieved February 21, 2017 (www.slobodnaevropa.org/a/zajednica-srpskih-opstina-nacekanju/27468934.html).

5

POLICING THE MEDITERRANEAN

The Use of Naval Forces in Immigration Enforcement

Jonathan Swarts

PURDUE UNIVERSITY NORTHWEST

> Recent years have seen a surge in the numbers of migrants and refugees taking to the sea in order to escape poverty and war for a new life in developed countries. This is particularly true at the epicenter of the current migration crisis: the Mediterranean. In seeking to cope with—and, indeed, to stem—large-scale migration to their shores, the EU and several European countries have utilized naval forces to patrol territorial waters, apprehend would-be migrants, and enforce immigration laws. In so doing, naval forces that have been trained largely for warfighting have increasingly been called upon to perform more constabulary duties, for which they may be neither well-trained nor equipped. This article examines these maritime migration flows and the implications of using military forces for immigration enforcement in an increasingly securitized environment.

The last several years have seen Europe's largest migration of people since the Second World War as hundreds of thousands of migrants fled war and unrest in the Middle East and beyond. However, a particularly salient fact is that this migration has occurred almost entirely by sea. With land borders more effectively controlled, and with air travel options strictly limited by security arrangements, the sea route has become the most utilized way for those desperate to arrive in Europe. The International Organization for Migration (IOM) estimates that in 2015, 1,046,599 migrants arrived in Europe, of whom 1,011,712—or 96.7 percent—arrived by sea (International Organization for Migration 2015). Since 2014, over 1.5 million migrants have traveled to Europe by sea, making this perhaps the largest human maritime movement in modern history.

The humanitarian effects of this movement, of course, have been dramatic and, at times, catastrophic. With huge numbers of people attempting to reach

Europe by either a short sea route from Turkey to Greece or a longer and more treacherous route from Libya to Italy and Malta, accounts of harrowing passages marked by overcrowded boats, rough seas, capsizings, and at times hundreds of drownings have become all too common.

This study analyzes the increasing militarization of the European response to the migration challenge. Focusing on the primarily maritime aspect of EU migration patterns in recent years, it illustrates how, just as the migration issue has been *securitized* in popular and official discourse, the actual "on the ground" response has become increasingly *militarized*. As migrant numbers exploded and as countries found themselves unable to effectively control migrant flows through traditional border methods, the focus shifted from a predominantly policing/border control approach to a much more militarized one, with ever greater levels of military capability being deployed and with national militaries increasingly called upon to play a constabulary role in immigration enforcement.

The article begins with a discussion of the changing role of military forces as they increasingly engage in such non-traditional tasks as the policing of migration. With the end of the Cold War and a decline in the perception of external threat, many countries have begun to rely to an ever greater extent on using military forces in non-traditional roles. It considers how the line between traditional military roles and other more policing-oriented constabulary duties has become increasingly blurred—and analyzes the challenge thus posed to both militaries and governments. The article then examines this trend in Europe, particularly the use of naval forces, by focusing on the efforts of individual countries and the European Union over the past several years to address the maritime challenge in the central and eastern Mediterranean. As large numbers of migrants began to attempt the crossing from North Africa to Italy, efforts were made first by Italy, then by the European Union, to rescue those in distress and to disrupt the activities of smugglers. More recently, the eastern Aegean became the route of choice for migrants from Syria and beyond via Turkey. With over a million migrants arriving on the Greek islands in the last year, attention has also focused on patrolling the relatively narrow straits separating Greece from Turkey, a task more recently taken up by a NATO force as well. In each case, the pattern was similar: initial efforts at controlling migration flows failed, to be replaced with increasing levels of militarization as a response.

The Changing Role of Military Forces

The question of the proper use of military forces has recently seen a resurgence in the scholarly literature. In a sense, this renewed attention is somewhat curious. Militaries have for centuries played a variety of "civil support" roles, from domestic policing and internal security to humanitarian assistance and disaster relief (Clarke 2014: 11–23). As Huntington points out in regard to the U.S. military, there was hardly a time in American history when the military did not play a significant role in a wide variety of non-military tasks, particularly in the nineteenth century before the rise of the United States as a global power (1993). While the *raison d'être* of the military has always been the defense of the homeland from foreign attack (Huntington 1993: 11), the reality has been that militaries have frequently played an important part in the national development of their countries' societies, industries, and physical infrastructure.

Despite this history, however, many scholars argue that the period of the Cold War had the effect of narrowing the focus of many Western militaries to the more fundamental task of national defense. Militaries continued to perform a variety of tasks—from disaster relief to direct political intervention, in some states—but the challenge of the Cold War focused, as it were, the attention of many militaries on how best to accomplish their "core" task of national defense from external threat.

Given this focus on defense of the state, a more traditional distinction between the military and police seemed to hold true. In contrast to the police's mission to "protect and serve," the job of the military is to "overwhelm and defeat" (Campbell and Campbell 2010: 329; see also Huntington 1957). Particularly when compared to police forces, military personnel are trained to use the maximum coercive force available to them in order to overwhelm and defeat the enemy (Pion-Berlin 2016: 2–3; Lutterbeck 2004). While the use of force may be seen by policy-makers as a last resort, when called upon to use force, military leaders generally prefer to use it as thoroughly and completely as possible. In direct contrast to police forces, militaries are generally equipped with the deadliest and most sophisticated weaponry that can be afforded, with the goal of using this weaponry to maximum possible effect on the enemy in order to achieve victory.

In contrast, police have traditionally been charged with maintaining public order and safety within national boundaries. Within this fundamentally inward-looking orientation, they are trained to use the most effective minimal level of force and coercion—ideally, relying on consent and trust—in the maintenance of public safety and the enforcement of laws. An emphasis is placed on personal interaction and integration with the publics they serve, with force being used as a last resort, and only then on a spectrum of coercion that only gradually moves to higher levels. Moreover, police equipment and weapons have traditionally been limited to the minimum amount necessary (with some police forces lightly armed, if at all)—with the goal of police work being to use the minimum force necessary to maintain public order and safety (Kleinig 1996; Miller et al. 1997). In short, police and military forces have been traditionally distinct—with distinct missions, training, equipment, and doctrines regarding the use of force (see Greener-Barcham 2007; Weiss 2012). As Paul Shemella puts it, "The classic and preferred role for armed forces is to defend a nation from external attack; the only role for the police is to enforce laws" (2006: 124).

The end of the superpower rivalry that characterized the Cold War, however, led many to question these traditional distinctions—and, indeed, for some to question the need for, or purpose of, the military in places now seemingly far removed from external threat. The end of the Cold War "removed the dominant strategic lens through which armed forces were developed and understood, and has entailed a fundamental reconsideration of their purpose and the basis [of their] legitimacy" (Edmunds 2006: 1062). This has been particularly true as the clear objective of state security vis-à-vis foreign aggression has been transformed into a much wider and more diffuse set of concerns. As Lutterbeck puts it,

> there now seems to be relatively broad agreement that the main security risks facing the countries of the Euro-Atlantic area since the end of bipolarity, apart from threats posed by so-called rogue states, are no longer state-based and military but rather non-state and transnational, consisting in various illicit or uncontrolled cross-border phenomena at the sub-state level (2004: 51).

Thus, as the external threats seemed to recede, they came to be replaced by newer security concerns. The security focus broadened to include such threats as failed states, internal disorder, poverty, economic crisis, disease, environmental degradation and climate change, transnational crime, terrorism, and irregular immigration (Schnabel and Hristov 2010: 74; Buzan 1991, 1997; Wæver 1993; Buzan et al. 1998).

With this blurring of the lines between traditional and new threats, some argue that modern militaries must retool if they are to meet these threats—and indeed if they are to justify their own existence. It is in such cases that militaries are increasingly being called upon to perform constabulary duties. In fact, for some countries, the primary "role of the armed forces is no longer defense of the homeland . . . but rather to constitute a force in being for carrying out a much broader range of missions, tasks, and functions" (Clarke 2014: 43; see also Lutterbeck 2004: 46).

The consequence of this coincidence of internal and external threats—or rather the interpenetration of the two—is said to be the blurring of the lines between traditional police and military roles and duties. On the one hand, police forces in many places have been increasingly militarized (Clarke 2014: 50–3). Particularly in places like the U.S.-Mexico border, police have become much more like paramilitaries, with weapons, training, tactics, and self-perceptions that more closely resemble soldiers fighting in a war zone than police officers walking a city beat (Dunn 1996; Slack et al. 2016). On the other hand, militaries have been increasingly called upon to perform duties that traditionally have been more associated with policing—assisting in disaster relief, attacking criminal gangs and drug traffickers, engaging in peacekeeping and nation-building operations in foreign countries (activities that often involve significant policing duties and training of police forces), and, as discussed in this article, attempting to control irregular migration (Edmunds 2006). While some countries have strengthened existing paramilitary-style forces—or created new forces—to exercise these duties (Lutterbeck 2006; Schnabel and Hristov 2010: 78), many countries have seen their active-duty army and naval forces assuming these roles. This article actually highlights the increasing interaction between policing and the military—as coast guards of EU member states and such paramilitary forces as the Spanish *Guardia Civil* and the Italian *Guardia di Finanza* have been joined by these countries' navies, and now the maritime assets of NATO, in dealing with the migration crisis.

Whether the increased participation of military forces is ultimately detrimental to society—and the military itself—is a matter of some debate. On the one hand, scholars have identified a range of potential problems when militaries take on roles traditionally performed by civilians (Shemella 2006: 139: Pion-Berlin and Trinkunas 2005: 5, 7–8; Schnabel and Hristov 2010: 79; Kapucu 2011: 22). A short list would include:

1. The diversion of militaries from their primary focus on war fighting.
2. Confusion within society over "who's in charge" or who *should be* "in charge."
3. Heightened expectations of what the military can do in tasks it is not well equipped or trained to do—and a potential subsequent loss of credibility if it fails.
4. The militarization of policing and civil society.
5. The politicization of the military.
6. A sense of military entitlement and/or actual military autonomy in national policy-making.
7. Human rights violations by a force trained for combat and the application of violence, not de-escalation and policing.

Particularly when it comes to border policing, many fear that the "militarization of the police" and the assumption of police roles by the military has the effect of escalating the potential lethality of encounters between migrants and authorities, endangering lives on all sides, intimidating already desperate migrants with the sight of troops or warships, and posing a serious threat to civil liberties. Moreover, in countries where the line between police and military forces has often been an ambiguous one—in Latin America, for example, particularly under authoritarian regimes—the cross-fertilization of these two forces is often seen as inimical to democratization and the protection of civil liberties (Desch 1999). For these critics, the closer integration, or functional crossover, between the military and the police weakens both institutions—detracting from the police's proper focus on minimally coercive public safety and law enforcement and from the military's proper concern with external defense through the use of lethal force.

Despite these concerns, others argue that such changes are not only part of the new world of blurred security, but also are not inherently detrimental to either police or the military, nor to the societies they serve. For a start, militaries continue to be called upon to perform tasks for which civilian forces are inadequate. Extraordinary circumstances such as natural disasters, internal insurrection, economic crisis or sudden, massive migration may bring out the military as the only force with the capability to respond effectively (Schnabel and Hristov 2010: 77; Schnabel and Krupanski 2014: 130). These one-off cases of military intervention "are designed to enhance the capacity of civilian security providers" and, as long as they are of limited extent and duration, do not unduly blur the line between the military and police (Schnabel and Krupanski 2014: 119; Shemella 2006: 130–1).

Moreover, even in more sustained cases of the military performing constabulary roles, some contend that there is not an *ipso facto* danger of military overreach. For example, in a study of the use of military forces in combatting drug cartel kingpins, Pion-Berlin (2016) argues that in "high-value" targeted operations where the tactical requirements and operational details closely align with military training and assets, military forces can be used successfully (see also Pion-Berlin and Trinkunas 2005; Pion-Berlin and Arcenaux 2000). In fact, many militaries increasingly see constabulary actions as part of the role description of the "post-modern military." While constabulary functions are often viewed by many soldiers as less rewarding personally, less likely to lead to promotion, and as a distraction from their "real" jobs (Segal et al. 1998; Janowitz 1983), others have argued that properly trained soldiers can effectively perform constabulary duties. In fact, as security environments change, as do the demands placed on modern militaries, these duties should be embraced as appropriate and worthwhile (Wass de Czege 2006; McLennan 2002). This is particularly true of immigration enforcement—a kind of halfway point between external defense and internal security that Schnabel and Krupanski refer to as the "hybridity of border control" (2014: 125). It is also more likely in countries whose militaries are focused less on global power projection and expeditionary war fighting and more on homeland security, border patrol, and internal policing (for a typology of these roles see Shemella 2006). In these cases, constabulary operations can be nearly a *raison d'être* of a country's military—and should not be seen *a priori* as inherently problematic. Given these widespread shifts in the role and mission of militaries, the transformation of the migration response in the Mediterranean is particularly important.

As will be seen in the next section, the challenge of migration by sea has come to be increasingly addressed by heavier and more lethal military forces. What seems to have begun as an expedient reaction by public officials overwhelmed by the scale and sudden emergence of mass migration by sea to the EU's borders has now taken a much more permanent character, as these operations have been moved to the external security apparatus of EU policy, and as the EU has sought (and received) UN Security Council authorization to conduct operations far in excess of territorial defense.

Mediterranean Migration by Sea

While the dramatic—and often tragic—scenes of hundreds of thousands of migrants crowding boats bound for Europe in 2015 and 2016 were, in many ways, of unprecedented scope and scale, Europe has in fact been the target destination of millions of migrants since the early 1990s. Then, as now, large numbers of these migrants attempted sea crossings to Europe. Thus, while the locations of these crossings have changed, as have the sheer numbers of those attempting them, the fact of maritime migration to Europe is not particularly new.

Specifically, in the early 1990s, Italy and Spain found themselves the desired destinations of tens of thousands of would-be migrants. With the collapse of Communism in Eastern Europe, and Albania in particular, the Adriatic Sea crossing from Albania to Italy became the route of choice for migrants coming from Albania, Turkey, Iraq, and beyond. At the same time, the narrow crossing at the Strait of Gibraltar emerged as a preferred route for thousands of sub-Saharan Africans attempting to reach Europe. The numbers, while small compared to current trends, were nonetheless significant: in 1997, approximately 30,000 undocumented migrants arrived in Italy from Albania and, by 2000, Spanish authorities were intercepting nearly 800 vessels a year in Spanish waters, with over 15,000 people detained (Lutterbeck 2006: 62, 63, 76).

The response was the activation of paramilitary—and later, military forces. Both Italy and Spain relied on their paramilitary gendarmeries—the *Guardia di Finanza* and *Guardia Civil*, respectively—to combat illegal migration (see Lutterbeck 2004, 2013; Clark 2014: 127–8). As Lutterbeck discusses, these paramilitary forces, equipped with sophisticated sensors, military-style weaponry, and significant naval and air assets, represented an early, clearly militarized response to the migration crisis (2006). Moreover, the resources allocated to these forces increased dramatically in response to Mediterranean migration with, for example, the *Guardia di Finanza*'s budget nearly tripling over the course of the 1990s, with significant upgrades to both its air and naval capabilities (Lutterbeck 2008: 2). However, this was but a prelude to the involvement of these countries' respective national navies, particularly the Italian navy. Finding that the resources of the historically more policing-oriented gendarmeries were insufficient given the burgeoning scale of migration, the large geographical size of the Mediterranean involved, and the need to operate beyond territorial waters, the Italian, Spanish, and (eventually) other European navies became active in migration policing and anti-smuggling operations. This period saw the significant engagement of warships in patrolling borders, apprehending people smugglers, detaining migrants, and combating illegal drugs and other crimes. In the case of the Italian *Marina Militare*, for instance, by the early 2000s, about one-quarter of the navy's time at sea was being devoted to immigration control (Lutterbeck 2006: 67).

The engagement of national navies in immigration enforcement marked an important turning point both operationally and conceptually. Operationally, navies have brought to immigration enforcement a range of technical capabilities—particularly surveillance and detection equipment—beyond the scope of their countries' coast guards and gendarmeries. Conceptually—as will be discussed in more detail below—the use of military forces at sea reflected a decided shift in the direction of the securitization—then, the increasing militarization—of the migration issue. Throughout the 1990s, migration became an important political issue in many southern European societies, with the social and political response to the sudden (and largely unexpected) surge of migration reflecting a "securitized" interpretation of migration as posing a substantial, existential threat to the state and society—one comparable to a threat posed by an external military force (Swarts and Karakatsanis 2012). This securitized interpretation of migration at the level of political discourse came to be matched "on the ground" by an increasingly militarized response. The initial response by Italy and others to migration in the 1990s should be understood from this perspective—as military assets intended to combat external armed threats began to be deployed to counter the new security "threat" of uncontrolled migration (Lutterbeck 2006).

This national response to the migration challenge increasingly came to be linked to a larger EU-based response. Recognizing the inability of single countries to effectively combat illegal migration, particularly over the large area of the Mediterranean, as well as the fact that many migrants were actually seeking to transit through their country of arrival to points in northern Europe, the European Union began in the first decade of the 2000s to develop multilateral maritime operations engaged in the surveillance, detection, interception, and rescue of irregular migrants. Many of these efforts were (and are) coordinated by Frontex, the EU border protection organization established in 2005. This agency utilizes the technological and equipment assets of member states to provide assistance to countries in policing the borders of the European Union. In the early 2000s, the maritime efforts of Frontex focused on three main migration routes across the Mediterranean: a western route between Morocco, the Canary Islands, and Spain, the central route between Libya and Italy/Malta, and the eastern route between Turkey and Greece. While there were a large number of Frontex efforts in this period, several operations in particular deserve mention.

One of the first of these Frontex operations was Operation Hera, begun in 2006. This operation focused primarily on stemming irregular migration from Africa to Spain via the Canary Islands. This involved, among other things, surveillance in the territorial waters of Senegal and Mauritania (with these countries' consent) by aircraft and ships from Spain, Italy, Portugal, and Finland. This operation was deemed a success, as the number of undocumented migrants arriving in the Canaries dropped by at least half from 2006 to 2007 (House of Lords 2008), and led to a series of similar operations, both large and small, focused on the three main migrant routes. Overall, the number crossing on the West African route dropped from 31,600 in 2006 to only 200 in 2010 (Frontex, "Western African Route" n.d.).

The central Mediterranean route between North Africa and Malta was the focus of Operation Nautilus, launched in 2007. This operation focused on disrupting the flow of migrants from Libya to Malta, a flow generally facilitated by human smugglers and their networks. This operation, which involved nine EU states, utilized ten ships, three helicopters and four fixed-wing aircraft, claimed the detection of 3,173 undocumented migrants (House of Lords 2008). However, this operation was unable to duplicate the success of Operation Hera in the Canaries. With a much larger sea area in question, and without the cooperation of the Libyan government to stop the departure of boats or to allow Frontex operations in its territorial waters, the boats continued to come—many changing, based on apparently good intelligence possessed by smugglers, their original destination of Malta to the Italian island of Lampedusa (Frontex, "Frontex in the Mediterranean" n.d.). Presaging a problem that would become very common in recent years, Ilkka Laitenen, the head of Frontex, admitted that the very presence of Frontex may have served to attract more migrant boats. Traffickers quickly learned to have migrants approach Frontex patrols in Italian or Maltese waters and sink their boats deliberately so as to be saved and taken ashore (*Times of Malta* 2008). In the end, the numbers attempting the central Mediterranean crossing fluctuated based on changing political developments in Libya until the dramatic upsurge of 2014–15 (Frontex, "Central Mediterranean Route" n.d.).

In the eastern Mediterranean in this "early" period, the route from Turkey to Greece, both by land across the Evros River and by sea to the eastern Aegean islands, proved the most popular. With an average of over 51,000 yearly arrivals from 2008 to 2011, the eastern route consistently ranked above the other routes during this period. As in the other cases, Frontex was at the forefront of border protection action on this route, primarily through Operation Poseidon, which ran in several forms from 2006 to 2015. Initially set up as a border patrol and surveillance operation in the Aegean Sea, the operation developed a land component in 2010, as large numbers of migrants—over 300 a day in late 2010— attempted to cross from Turkey into Greece along the short border formed by the Evros River (Frontex, "Eastern Mediterranean Route" n.d.). The operation on land involved for the first time the insertion of an emergency Rapid Border Intervention Team (RABIT) of over 200 Frontex agents from 26 countries to patrol the border and provide surveillance and technical expertise lacking at the local level (Sofia News Agency 2011). As a further response, in 2011 the Greek government completed a 10.4-kilometer long fence to cover an area where the Evros does not form part of the Greek-Turkish border. The effect—again, one that would be repeated countless times during the much greater surges of 2014–16—was to push the migrant flow elsewhere. While the fence and increased patrols had the effect of reducing land crossings by as much as 90 percent, it also appeared to push the migrant flow to a much more dangerous place: the sea. Whereas, in 2011, 98 percent of apprehensions of undocumented migrants took place on land, by 2013, 94 percent of apprehensions took place at sea.[1]

In short, the period from the 1990s to 2013 was a period in which European countries and the EU itself saw a significant rise in migration attempts from North Africa, the Middle East, and beyond, largely across the Mediterranean. It was also the period in which various operations against illegal migration and human smuggling were launched—several of which have been noted here. In each of these cases, the dominant logic was the enforcement of migration laws, the deterrence of illegal migration, and the apprehension of undocumented migrants and human traffickers. As the numbers of migrants increased, however, the sense of a security threat did as well. In turn, the securitized sense of threat produced an increasingly militarized policy response. Individual states and later the EU—primarily through Frontex—began to respond to these "threats," increasing levels of military assets and potential firepower. As discussed earlier, the Italian *Guardia di Finanza* dramatically increased its reach and capability over the 1990s—going from 330 boats, 68 helicopters, and 0 airplanes in 1989 to 582 boats, 96 helicopters, and 14 airplanes in 1999, while its operating budget would nearly triple over the same period (Lutterbeck 2006: 65–6). The capabilities of the *Guardia Civil* were also greatly enhanced over this period. While not seeing the level of budget growth as that in Italy, the specifically maritime assets of the *Guardia Civil* went from 0 naval personnel and 0 boats in 1985 to 728 naval personnel and 50 boats in 2000 (Lutterbeck 2006: 67). Meanwhile, the annual budget of Frontex went from €6.3 million in 2005 to nearly €88 million in 2010—nearly 14 times higher in only five years (Morehouse and Blomfield 2011: 3)—and was projected to reach €320 million in 2017 (*Ekathimerini* 2016).

The Migration Explosion and Increased Militarization

Throughout the early 2000s, particularly as the result of war in Iraq, Afghanistan, and Syria, large numbers of people continued to attempt to migrate to Europe. Estimates from 2004 were that 100,000 to 120,000 asylum seekers crossed the Mediterranean to Europe (Lutterbeck 2006: 61). Large as these numbers were, however, they would be dwarfed by the massive upsurge that began in 2015, particularly as the war in Syria began to produce large numbers of refugees. Specifically, arrivals of irregular migrants in 2014 numbered 283,532, up from 107,365 in 2013. However, in 2015, as mentioned previously, 1,046,599 arrivals took place. (See Table 5.1.) Of particular note is the explosion in arrivals by sea. Between 2013 and 2015, the central route between North Africa and Italy went from 45,298 to 153,852 arrivals—itself a dramatic increase in the number of people attempting this route. However, the eastern route in the Aegean

TABLE 5.1 Irregular Arrivals to Europe

	2013	2014	2015	2016
Total Arrivals	107,365	283,532	1,046,599	387,739
Of whom:				
Western Mediterranean Sea	2,609	4,755	3,845	8,162
Central Mediterranean Sea	45,298	170,664	153,842	181,436
Eastern Mediterranean Sea	11,831	44,057	853,650	173,614
Eastern Mediterranean Land	12,968	6,777	3,713	3,292

Sources: Frontex, *Annual Risk Analysis 2015*: 16; International Organization for Migration (2015: 5, 2016b: 6, 2016a).

exploded—from 11,831 arrivals in 2013 to 44,057 in 2014 to 853,650 in 2015. Greece thus became the focus of one of the largest maritime migrations in modern history. In October 2015 alone, well over 200,000 migrants made the passage from Turkey to the Greek islands—that is, nearly as many migrants to the islands in one month than the entire EU received in all of 2014 (IOM 2015: 3).

This surge of migration, as well as several cases of hundreds of migrants drowning on the central route, gradually led to a shift towards the increased use of military assets and military forces both in conducting search and rescue (SAR) operations, as well as in policing and border protection work. This trend is clear in regard to both the Central and Eastern Mediterranean route.

Naval Forces in the Central Mediterranean

The evolution of the use of military forces in the recent migration crisis can be traced most clearly to the rise in migrant numbers discussed above, as well as two shipwrecks of migrant boats off the Italian coast in 2013 that dramatically raised the public profile of the dangers of the central route and led to more concerted, and more military-oriented, action.

While the shipwreck of overcrowded and unseaworthy migrant boats was not a new phenomenon—hundreds, for instance, had drowned near the Libyan coast in the spring of 2009—the October 2013 shipwreck of two migrant boats just off the coast of Lampedusa brought the issue home with an immediacy born of proximity. In these wrecks—on 3 and 11 October 2013—more than 600 migrants drowned as their boats capsized in Italian and Maltese waters, respectively.

The response of the Italian government was the creation of a naval search and rescue program called Operation Mare Nostrum. This operation utilized vessels of the *Marina Militare* to patrol over 27,000 square miles in the Strait of Sicily. Over the course of the next year—from October 2013 to 2014—the Italian government deployed five surface ships (one amphibious ship, two frigates, and two corvettes/patrollers), two submarines, and a variety of helicopters and patrol aircraft in combination with over 900 military personnel. While the aim of the operation was ostensibly to enforce maritime security and combat such illegal activities as human trafficking, it also had the effect of being a significant SAR operation. The Italian Ministry of Defense estimated that 150,810 migrants were rescued and 330 human smugglers arrested over the course of the one-year operation (Ministero della Difesa n.d.). The size and the cost of this operation, however, proved more than the Italian government was willing or able to bear. With a monthly cost of about €9 million, the total cost for the operation was €114 million, with the EU contributing only approximately €1.8 million (Capasso 2015). Given this, the Italian government—to the dismay of various human rights and migrant NGOs—terminated the program at the end of October 2014, to be replaced by Frontex's Operation Triton.

Operation Triton, however, differed in significant ways from Mare Nostrum. As opposed to Mare Nostrum's primary occupation with search and rescue, Triton was designed from the beginning as a border surveillance and border protection operation. Frontex argued that, in keeping with its mission as the EU's border protection institution, search and rescue was not its primary goal—and, therefore, it should not be seen as a replacement for Mare Nostrum at the EU level. As a border protection force—and not a SAR one—its range of operations was restricted to 30 miles off the Italian coast and its assets were reduced to one large ship and three small patrol boats, as opposed to the "five big ships" of Mare Nostrum (*Guardian* 2014).

The succeeding months, however, saw a sharp increase in deaths along the central route, with 1,686 migrants killed in the first four months of 2015 as opposed to 60 in the same period the previous year (IOM Missing Migrants Project n.d.). On 19 April alone, in perhaps the Mediterranean's worst civilian loss of life in recent times, over 800 would-be migrants were killed when their boat capsized off the coast of Libya (with only 28 survivors).

The reaction from the European Union took two forms. First, at an emergency summit held after the 19 April catastrophe, the EU tripled the funding to Frontex for the operation, bringing it up to levels spent by the Italian government on Mare Nostrum (*International Business Times* 2015). It also, without specifically expanding the mandate to include SAR operations, extended the patrol area to 138 nautical miles south of Sicily (Frontex 2015a) and increased the naval assets available to the force. This came to include such ships as HMS *Bulwark*, a 19,000-ton amphibious assault ship (and, at the time, the UK fleet flagship) with significant amphibious and helicopter capability. Moreover, the emergency summit's communiqué contained 17 proposals for strengthening the EU's response to the migrant crisis. Chief among them was to take a more proactive approach against the human smugglers—to "undertake systematic efforts to identify, capture, and destroy vessels before they are used by traffickers" (European Council 2015b).

This refocusing of efforts beyond border patrol and protection to the more outward-directed goal of *attacking* traffickers' vessels *before* they could be used was clearly a step towards a much more muscular, interventionist approach that would require military capabilities and military operations. This new objective of disrupting the traffickers' "business model" would lead directly to the second main consequence of the April 2015 humanitarian disaster—the creation of the European Union Naval Force Mediterranean (EUNAVFOR Med), often referred to as Operation Sophia. Very significantly, this new force was placed, not within the EU's border control apparatus, but rather was made a part of its military bureaucracy, the EU's Common Security and Defense Policy (CSDP). Moreover, the European Council characterized its response to human smuggling and trafficking as a *"military* crisis management operation" and placed strategic planning and operational control of the forces involved under the direction of the EU Military Committee (European Council 2015a, emphasis added; Tardy 2015: 3). In so doing, the Council intentionally placed EUNAVFOR Med outside the EU's normal policing and border patrol mechanisms, thereby launching a self-described military operation involving a higher level of coercive, military-based potential than has ever before been deployed in an EU mission.

This new operation was intended to be conducted in essentially four phases, the first two of which have already begun: 1) the deployment of military assets to the area of the central route; 2) the boarding, search, seizure, and destruction of vessels on the high seas suspected of human smuggling; 3) the extension of those search and seizure operations to the territorial waters of Libya and 4) the attacking of traffickers' assets and operations on the territory of Libya itself. This operation is highly significant both for its geographical reach and its legal authority for the use of force. Geographically, Operation Sophia covers a wide swathe of sea between Italy and Libya, amounting to about 525,000 square nautical miles (House of Lords 2016), an area over four times the land area of Italy itself. Moreover, the operation has a legal remit from both the EU and the United Nations that far exceeds the limited border protection goals of such operations as Triton. In October 2015, the UN Security Council passed resolution 2240, which authorized phase two of Operation Sophia—in which the EU is now authorized to board, search, and even destroy vessels on the high seas involved in human smuggling from Libya. These powers were further strengthened in June 2016 when Security Council Resolution 2249 authorized EUNAVFOR to assist in carrying out the UN arms embargo against ships on the high seas suspected of trading arms to Libya.

Clearly, Operation Sophia has reached a level of military participation both conceptually and operationally that is unprecedented for EU migration control efforts. Conceptually, the objectives of the EUNAVFOR are clearly oriented and well-suited to military forces: the search, seizure, and destruction of vessels and the enforcement of a UN arms embargo. Operationally, EUNAVFOR has seen the utilization of significant naval assets. Clearly revealing the fundamentally different nature of this operation as compared to that conducted by coastal patrol boats has been the presence in the force of the Italian aircraft carriers *Cavour* (the

Italian Navy's flagship) and *Garibaldi* and the fact that, in its first year, the operation utilized 19 ships, eight helicopters, eight fixed-wing aircraft, four submarines, and over 400 military personnel (European Union External Action 2016a).

Whether this rather significant deployment of military assets has been effective is a matter of debate—and somewhat beyond the scope of this article. EUNAVFOR Med reported in June 2016 that, as a result of Operation Sophia, 39 smugglers' boats had been destroyed, 71 suspected smugglers were arrested, 15,600 people were rescued in over 91 operations, and 32,334 people were rescued by others with help from Operation Sophia assets (European Union External Action 2016b). Others, however, point out that such operations usually have the effect of simply pushing the migration flow elsewhere and that, in this particular case, the destruction of smugglers' boats has encouraged a shift to cheap inflatable craft that smugglers are willing to see destroyed, but which are extremely unseaworthy and thus even more dangerous for migrants (House of Lords 2016). What is not disputed, however, is that the creation of EUNAVFOR Med represents a significant step in the direction of the securitization and militarization of the EU response on the central route. With top-notch naval assets conducting patrols, with an expanded remit to not only capture and destroy smuggling assets but to enforce a UN arms embargo, and with the operation firmly located in the international security institutions of the EU (as opposed to its border control apparatus), the shift to a much more muscular, activist, and militarized approach is apparent.

The Eastern Mediterranean Response

As discussed previously, the eastern route between Turkey and the Greek islands has seen by far the largest growth in the number of migrants attempting to reach Europe. Over the last few years, Greece has experienced the largest refugee crisis in Europe since the Second World War, as nearly a million migrants made their way across the eastern route in the Aegean.

While the scale of the movement of people to the Greek islands from 2014 to 2016 was wholly without precedent, Greece, as discussed above, had already seen significant numbers of people on the move in the previous decade and, indeed, since the 1990s and the collapse of Communism. In addition to various national attempts to regulate and control irregular migration, the newly created Frontex launched Operation Poseidon in Greece, beginning in 2006. This operation, comprised of both land and sea elements, aimed at securing the border, stemming migrant flows, and combating human smuggling. As discussed above, it played an important role in 2010 in attempting to stem the flow of migrants over the land border with Turkey, with the intervention of Frontex's first Rapid Border Intervention Team (RABIT), in addition to the Greek government's building of a fence along its Turkish border. Throughout this period, Frontex's Operation Poseidon Sea continued to patrol the straits of the Eastern Aegean in collaboration with the Greek Coast Guard and Navy.

The advent of the massive migrant flows of 2015, however, led to two developments to further strengthen these patrols—both of which represented a significant uptick in the level of naval presence dispatched to deal with migration in the Aegean. The first was in December 2015. Faced with overwhelming numbers of migrants arriving to the Greek islands, Frontex, at Greece's request, launched Operation Poseidon Rapid Intervention, replacing Joint Operation Poseidon Sea. This led to the immediate deployment of 293 Frontex officers on land to assist overwhelmed Greek authorities with the reception, identification, and processing of migrants, with a total of nearly 600 officers arriving by mid-2016 (European Commission 2016) (this number being significantly less, it should be pointed out, than the over 1600 guards the Greek government requested [*EUBulletin* 2016]). It also involved the deployment of 15 naval vessels from participating EU countries in order to assist with "unprecedented migratory pressure on the Greek borders" (Frontex 2015b).

The situation on the eastern route changed dramatically, however, in March 2016 with an agreement between the EU and Turkey to facilitate the deportation to Turkey of all irregular migrants who had made their way from Turkey to Greece. It stipulated, among other provisions, that, beginning on 20 March, all migrants to Greece from Turkey deemed inadmissible to the EU would be returned to Turkey. Moreover, for each Syrian returned to Turkey, another Syrian would be re-settled within the EU. The EU, Greece, and Turkey also pledged to work more closely in the Aegean to combat irregular migration. The effect on arrivals to Greece was immediate and dramatic. As Table 5.2 shows, the number of arrivals dropped from a 2016 high of 2,117 per day in February to less than 100 per day in May, June, and July.

The second major development in the Eastern Mediterranean—and one that clearly moved the policing of migration into a much more militarized

TABLE 5.2 Arrivals to Greece, 2016

	Average per day
January	2,248
February	1,984
March 1–8*	1,375
March 9–30**	701
April	131
May	47
June	70
July	66
August	122
September	109
October	103

* Before EU-Turkey Agreement
** After EU-Turkey Agreement

Source: International Organization for Migration (2016c).

position—was the first-ever direct involvement of NATO in helping police the migration crisis. In February 2016, as a result of requests for help from German Chancellor Angela Merkel and Turkish Prime Minister Ahmet Davutoğlu, NATO ordered its Standing NATO Maritime Group 2 (SNMG2) to the Aegean (Zhukov 2016). This decision arose in direct response to the demand of various NATO members—including Belgium, Germany, and particularly Turkey—to more fully and comprehensively respond to emerging threats on the alliance's southern flank, including terrorism and uncontrolled migration (Argano 2016). The mission of this first-ever NATO intervention in European migration is to provide surveillance and intelligence to Greek and Turkish authorities, as well as to Frontex, about boat movements and possible smuggling operations in the straits between the Greek islands and Turkey. NATO ships are not engaged in active policing of the straits, nor do they engage in SAR operations except as a last resort. Unlike EU operations such as Poseidon in the Aegean and Triton in the central Mediterranean, however, the NATO force is not limited to the high seas and the territorial waters of an EU state. It has the advantage of being able to operate in the territorial waters of both Greece and Turkey, and thus is able to provide more effective intelligence to Turkish forces in order to stop boats before reaching Greek—and EU—waters (Zhukov 2016).

The involvement of SNMG2 in the surveillance—though not interdiction—of irregular migration to Europe is a significant step in the involvement of a military and political alliance whose chief concern is international security and defense. Its patrols in the Aegean are conducted by warships of several NATO countries, not all of which are EU member states (e.g., the United States and Turkey). At the time of this writing, the force consists of ships from Germany, Canada, Albania, Romania, Spain, Greece, and Turkey, and is commanded by a German admiral. While no "shooting" or other incidents of military force have taken place during these patrols, the presence of NATO warships in the Eastern Aegean—as does the use of EU naval forces in the Central Mediterranean—clearly indicates that military forces and their accompanying heavy assets are likely to be a key part of the European approach to migration enforcement for some time to come.

Conclusion

This article has considered the expansion of the military's non-traditional roles by discussing the increasingly powerful naval forces that have been brought to bear in policing and attempting to suppress irregular migration in the Mediterranean. As the numbers of irregular migrants and asylum seekers grew over the past 20 years—and in particular in the last few years—European responses have increasingly focused on operations using military (as opposed to coast guard and border patrol) assets with an increased geographical range. As these operations increased in scope and scale, European navies became increasingly involved, to the extent that the EU force in the central Mediterranean is now engaged in the enforcement of a UN arms embargo, in addition to its primary mission to combat irregular migration. What had been an operation of domestic border control has been transformed into an operation intended to enforce—by military means—UN Security Council resolutions potentially involving the destruction of boats and the killing of smugglers. This represents a significant example of the blurred and overlapping roles played by militaries in such "hybrid" situations as border policing. It would seem, particularly with EUNAVFOR Med's task to enforce the Libyan arms embargo, that a line has been crossed from the policing focus on protecting and serving to the military's core job of "breaking things and hurting people" (Clarke 2014: 144). Meanwhile, a NATO task force patrols the Eastern Mediterranean to identify would-be migrants at sea. The introduction of a NATO naval mission in the Aegean, despite its limited mandate and scope of operations, is thus also indicative of this trend.

What this holds for the future of migration control efforts, as well as for the navies involved, remains to be seen. Trends towards the militarization of border control do not generally tend to reverse themselves, as seen in places like the US-Mexico border. Moreover, as militaries become more accustomed to constabulary assignments, and to the extent that their training and doctrine come to reflect these responsibilities, what has been seen as unusual and novel may come to be seen increasingly as part of the military's core mission in a world of blurred and interconnected challenges and perceived threats.

Note

1 Calculated from data in Angeli et al. (2014).

References

Angeli, Danai, Angeliki Dimitriadi, and Anna Triandafyllidou. 2014. "Assessing the Cost Effectiveness of Irregular Migration Control Policies in Greece." Athens: ELIAMEP. Retrieved July 8, 2016 (www.eliamep.gr/wp-content/uploads/2014/11/MIDAS-REPORT.pdf). P. 31.

Argano, Maria Elena. 2016. "A Stronger NATO Means a Stronger Europe: Sea Guardian and Operation Sophia Together." November 16. Retrieved February 8, 2017 (https://eulogos.blogactiv.eu/2016/11/15/a-stronger-nato-means-a-stronger-europe-sea-guardian-and-operation-sophia-together/).

Buzan, Barry. 1991. "New Patterns of Global Security in the Twenty-First Century." *International Affairs* 67(3):431–51.

Buzan, Barry. 1997. "Rethinking Security after the Cold War." *Cooperation and Conflict* 32(1):5–28.

Buzan, Barry, Ole Wæver, and Japp de Wilde, eds. 1998. *Security: A New Framework for Analysis*. London: Lynne Rienner.

Campbell, Donald J. and Kathleen M. Campbell. 2010. "Soldiers as Peace Officers/Police Offices as Soldiers: Role Evolution and Revolution in the United States." *Armed Forces and Society* 36(2):327–50.

Capasso, Alessia. 2015. "From Mare Nostrum to Triton: What Has Changed for Migrants?" Retrieved July 9, 2016 www.cafebabel.co.uk/society/article/from-mare-nostrum-to-triton-what-has-changed-for-migrants.html).

Clarke, John L. 2014. *What Should Armies Do? Armed Forces and Civil Security*. Farnham: Ashgate.

Desch, Michael C. 1999. *Civilian Control of the Military: The Changing Security Environment*. Baltimore: Johns Hopkins University Press.

Dunn, Timothy J. 1996. *The Militarization of the United States-Mexico Border, 1978–1992*. Austin, TX: University of Texas Press.

Edmunds, Timothy. 2006. "What *Are* the Armed Forces For? The Changing Nature of Military Roles in Europe." *International Affairs* 82(6):1059–75.

Ekathimerini. 2016. "Frontex Needs More Ships, Planes." February 23. Retrieved July 8, 2016 (www.ekathimerini.com/206253/article/ekathimerini/news/frontex-greece-needs-more-ships-planes).

EUBulletin. 2016. "'Poseidon Rapid' Intervention: Frontex Supports Surveillance of Greek Islands." January 4. Retrieved July 10, 2016 (http://eubulletin.com/5236-poseidon-rapid-intervention-frontex-supports-surveillance-of-greek-islands.html).

European Commission. 2016. "Implementing the EU-Turkey Statement: Questions and Answers." June 15. Retrieved July 10, 2016 (http://europa.eu/rapid/press-release_MEMO-16-1664_en.htm).

European Council. 2015a. "Council Decision (CFSP) 2015/778 of 18 May 2015 on a European Union Military Operation in the South Central Mediterranean (Eunavfor Med)." May 19. Retrieved February 8, 2017 (www.europarl.europa.eu/meetdocs/2014_2019/documents/libe/dv/4_council_decision_2015_778_/4_council_decision_2015_778_en.pdf).

European Council. 2015b. "Special Meeting of the European Council, 23 April 2015-Statement." April 23. Retrieved July 9, 2016 (www.consilium.europa.eu/en/press/press-releases/2015/04/23-special-euco-statement/).

European Union External Action. 2016a. "Eunavfor Med Operation Sophia: A New Force Commander after One Year at Sea." June 27. Retrieved July 9, 2016 (http://eeas.europa.eu/csdp/missions-and-operations/eunavfor-med/news/20160627_01_en.htm).

European Union External Action. 2016b. "New Hope for 816 People Rescued by Unafor MED Operation Sophia's Assets." June 10. Retrieved July 9, 2016 (http://eeas.europa.eu/csdp/missions-and-operations/eunavfor-med/news/20160610_01_en.htm.

Frontex. 2015a. "Frontex Expands its Joint Operation Triton." May 26. Retrieved July 9, 2016 (http://frontex.europa.eu/news/frontex-expands-its-joint-operation-triton-udpbHP).

Frontex. 2015b. "Frontex Launches Rapid Operational Assistance in Greece." December 29. Retrieved July 10, 2016 (http://frontex.europa.eu/news/frontex-launches-rapid-operational-assistance-in-greece-u3rqPy).

Frontex. n.d.a "Central Mediterranean Route." Retrieved July 8, 2016 (http://frontex.europa.eu/trends-and-routes/central-mediterranean-route/).

Frontex. n.d.b "Eastern Mediterranean Route." Retrieved July 8, 2016 (http://frontex.europa.eu/trends-and-routes/eastern-mediterranean-route/).

Frontex. n.d.c "Frontex in the Mediterranean." Retrieved July 8, 2016 (http://w2eu.net/frontex/frontex-in-the-mediterranean/.

Frontex. n.d.d "Western African Route." Retrieved July 8, 2016 (http://frontex.europa.eu/trends-and-routes/western-african-route/).

Greener-Barcham, B.K. 2007. "Crossing the Green or Blue Line? Exploring the Military-Police Divide." *Small Wars and Insurgencies* 18(1):90–112.

Guardian. 2014. "Italy: End of Ongoing Sea Rescue Mission 'Puts Thousands at Risk'." October 31. Retrieved July 9, 2016 (www.theguardian.com/world/2014/oct/31/italy-sea-mission-thousands-risk).

House of Lords. 2008. *Select Committee on European Union, Ninth Report, 2008.* Retrieved July 8, 2016 (www.publications.parliament.uk/pa/ld200708/ldselect/ldeucom/60/6008.htm).

House of Lords. 2016. "Select Committee on European Union, Operation Sophia, the EU's Naval Mission in the Mediterranean: An Impossible Challenge." May 13. Retrieved July 9, 2016 (www.publications.parliament.uk/pa/ld201516/ldselect/ldeucom/144/14406.htm).

Huntington, Samuel P. 1957. *The Solider and the State.* Cambridge, MA: Belknap Press.

Huntington, Samuel P. 1993. "New Contingencies, Old Roles." *Joint Forces Quarterly* 34:6–11.

International Business Times. 2015. "EU to Triple Funding to 'Operation Triton' to Tackle Mediterranean Migrant Crisis." April 24. Retrieved July 9, 2016 (www.ibtimes.co.uk/eu-triple-funding-operation-triton-tackle-mediterranean-migrant-crisis-1498100).

International Organization for Migration. 2015. *Mixed Migration Flows in the Mediterranean and Beyond.* Retrieved July 6, 2016 (http://doe.iom.int/docs/Flows%20Compilation%202015%20Overview.pdf).

International Organization for Migration. 2016a. "Migration Flows: Europe." Retrieved November 21, 2016 (http://migration.iom.int/europe/).

International Organization for Migration. 2016b. *Mixed Migration Flows in the Mediterranean and Beyond.* Retrieved February 8, 2017 (http://migration.iom.int/docs/2016_Flows_to_Europe_Overview.pdf).

International Organization for Migration. 2016c. *Mixed Migration Flows in the Mediterranean and Beyond: Compilation of Available Data and Information,* November 3–16, 2016–November 17, 2016. Retrieved November 21, 2016 (http://migration.iom.int/docs/WEEKLY_Flows_Compilation_No29_17_November_2016.pdf).

International Organization for Migration, Missing Migrants Project. n.d. "Mediterranean." Retrieved July 9, 2016 (http://missingmigrants.iom.int/mediterranean).

Janowitz, Morris. 1983. "Civil Consciousness and Military Performance." Pp. 55–80 in Morris Janowitz and Stephen D. Westbrook, eds. *The Political Education of Soldiers.* Beverly Hills: Sage.

Kapucu, Naim. 2011. "The Role of the Military in Disaster Response in the U.S." *European Journal of Economic and Political Studies* 4(2):7–33.

Kleinig, John. 1996. *The Ethics of Policing.* Cambridge: Cambridge University Press.

Lutterbeck, Derek. 2004. "Between Police and Military: The New Security Agenda and the Rise of Gendarmeries." *Cooperation and Conflict* 39(1):45–68.

Lutterbeck, Derek. 2006. "Policing Migration in the Mediterranean." *Mediterranean Politics* 11(1):59–82.

Lutterbeck, Derek. 2008. *Coping with Europe's Boat People: Trends and Policy Dilemmas in Controlling the EU's Mediterranean Borders.* Policy Brief 76 (February). Milan: Instituto per Gli Studi di Politica Internazionale.

Lutterbeck, Derek. 2013. *The Paradox of Gendarmeries: Between Expansion, Demilitarization and Dissolution.* Geneva: Geneva Centre for the Democratic Control of Armed Forces.

McLennan, Bruce. 2002. "The Marine Constabulary Role in Australia: Threat or Opportunity?" *Maritime Studies* 125:5–14.

Miller, Seumas, John Blackler, and Andrew Alexander. 1997. *Police Ethics.* St. Leonards, NSW: Allen and Unwin.

Ministero della Difesa. n.d. "Mare Nostrum Operation." Retrieved July 9, 2016 (www.marina.difesa.it/EN/operations/Pagine/MareNostrum.aspx).

Morehouse, Christal and Michael Blomfield. 2011. *Irregular Migration in Europe.* Washington, DC: Migration Policy Institute.
Pion-Berlin, David. 2016. "A Tale of Two Missions: Mexican Military Policy Patrols Versus High-Value Targeted Operations." *Armed Forces and Society,* forthcoming.
Pion-Berlin, David and Craig Arcenaux. 2000. "Decision-Makers or Decision-Takers? Military Missions and Civilian Control in Democratic South America." *Armed Forces and Society* 26(3):413–36.
Pion-Berlin, David and Harold Trinkunas. 2005. "Democratization, Social Crisis and the Impact of Military Domestic Roles in Latin America." *Journal of Political and Military Sociology* 33(1):5–24.
Schnabel, Albrecht and Danail Hristov. 2010. "Conceptualising Non-Traditional Roles and Tasks of Armed Forces." *Sicherheit und Frieden (S+F)* 28(2):73–80.
Schnabel, Albrecht and Marc Krupanski. 2014. "Evolving Internal Roles of the Armed Forces." *Prism* 4(4):119–37.
Segal, David R., Brian J. Reed, and David E. Rohall. 1998. "Constabulary Attitudes of National Guard and Regular Soldiers in the U.S. Army." *Armed Forces and Society* 24(4):535–48.
Shemella, Paul. 2006. "The Spectrum of Roles and Missions of the Armed Forces." Pp. 122–42 in Thomas C. Bruneau and Scott D. Tollefson, eds. *Who Guards the Guardians and How: Democratic Civil-Military Relations.* Austin: University of Texas Press.
Slack, Jeremy, Daniel E. Martínez, Allison Elizabeth Lee, and Scott Whiteford. 2016. "The Geography of Border Militarization: Violence, Death and Health in Mexico and the United States." *Journal of Latin American Geography* 15(1):7–32.
Sofia News Agency. 2011. "Frontex Mission in Greece Turns Permanent, Expanded to Bulgaria-Turkey Border." March 3. Retrieved July 8, 2016 (www.novinite.com/articles/125859/Frontex+Mission+in+Greece+Turns+Permanent,+Expanded+to+Bulgaria-Turkey+Border).
Swarts, Jonathan and Neovi M. Karakatsanis. 2012. "The Securitization of Migration: Greece in the 1990s." *Journal of Near Eastern and Balkan Studies* 14(1):33–51.
Tardy, Thierry. 2015. "Operation Sophia: Tackling the Refugee Crisis with Military Means." Paris: European Union Institute for Security Studies, September.
Times of Malta. 2008. "Frontex Chief Admits Failure." September 21. Retrieved July 8, 2016 (www.timesofmalta.com/articles/view/20080921/local/frontex-chief-admits-failure.225630).
Wæver, Ole. 1993. "Social Security: The Concept." In Ole Wæver, Barry Buzan, Morten Kelstrup, and Pierre Lemaitre, eds. *Identity, Migrations and the New Security Agenda in Europe.* New York: St. Martin's Press.
Wass de Czege, Huba. 2006. "On Policing the Frontiers of Freedom." *Army Magazine* 56(7):14–22.
Weiss, Tomáš. 2012. "Fighting Wars or Controlling Crowds? The Case of the Czech Military Forces and the Possible Blurring of Police and Military Functions." *Armed Forces and Society* 39(3):450–66.
Zhukov, Yuri M. 2016. "NATO's Mediterranean Mission." *Foreign Affairs,* February 21. Retrieved July 10, 2016 (www.foreignaffairs.com/articles/europe/2016-02-21/natos-mediterranean-mission).

6

ITALY AND THE REFUGEE CRISIS

The Humanitarian Dilemma

Francesca Longo

UNIVERSITY OF CATANIA

Political and Military Sociology: An Annual Review, 2017, Vol. 45: 91–105.

This article provides an analysis of Italian refugee policy in the last three decades and it argues that, since 2013, Italy has partially changed its approach on this topic, moving from a full "securitization" paradigm to one that is based on the notion of "human security." The first section focuses on the emergence of a "refugee issue" in Italy and on the Italian response. The second section shows the relevance of the European Union's migration and refugee policy to Italy, and the implications of the developing EU migration regime for Italian policy. The third section shows how the 2013 tragedies at sea acted as focusing events to catalyze significant policy changes at both the Italian and European Union levels. As a result, Italy has begun to play a significant role in shaping policy change in the EU.

Introduction

As highlighted in several articles of this volume, migration emerged as a security issue after the Cold War. In the 1990s, the transformation of the global security regime and the disappearance of the bipolar security framework altered both the nature and the perception of this issue. Specifically, while migration was previously considered a social and economic issue, since the end of the bipolar cleavage it has primarily been treated as a security issue. As a result, the migration-security nexus (Huysmans and Squire 2009) has been incorporated into this broader redefinition of the concept of security. The analysis of migration for security studies has mainly been affected by two theoretical approaches.

The first is the securitization approach, which applies the "securitization process" to the study of immigration policies based on the definition of mass migration as "an existential threat requiring emergency measures and justifying actions outside the normal bounds of political procedure" (Buzan et al. 1998). This approach produces a security-centered immigration and refugee policy focused primarily on the physical control of borders.

The second approach, which emphasizes humanitarian concerns, is focused on the relevance of transnational migration flows to *human* security, intended to protect "the vital interests of persons and communities" (Mascia 2011; Vietti and Scribner 2013). This approach results in immigration policy outputs that aim to respect international standards of human rights with a high level of guarantees for migrants and refugees.

In light of these two theoretical approaches, this article seeks to analyze the response of Italian institutions and leaders to the arrival of irregular migrants and asylum seekers since the 1990s. Beginning with the assumption that theoretical approaches affect the quality of policy outputs, this analysis will demonstrate the progression of two different models of refugee crisis management that were followed by Italy from the 1990s to the present. The first model, based on the securitization approach, produced policy measures that strengthened border control and increased the return of refugees to countries of origin. The second model, introduced in 2013 and partially based on the humanitarian approach, produced policy measures that were more oriented towards humanitarian intervention.

The article begins by briefly presenting the emergence and development of the refugee crisis in Italy and the Italian policy response up to the early 2000s. The second section focuses on the relationship between Italian and EU policy in regards to immigration, asylum, and border controls and checks. The final section of the article analyzes the transformation of Italian migration policy from one of security to a humanitarian approach, which was the result of tragedy, specifically, the migrant shipwreck that occurred near the Italian island of Lampedusa in 2013. In that section, the article stresses the role that Italy is attempting to play in revising EU policy on migrants and asylum seekers.

The Refugee Crisis in Italy: The Security Approach

The increase of arrivals of people fleeing their countries of origin due to fear for their personal safety or from poverty has become a major challenge for European states in the last ten years. Indeed, since early 2011, a series of global events acted as push factors, increasing the number of people moving towards Europe in search of safety or subsistence. The Arab uprisings and their predictable and unpredictable outcomes (in terms of change in the domestic politics of Arab states as well as in the political framework of the Middle East) changed the structure of migration flows, as mass movements of people in search of personal safety complemented the traditional economic migration flows. Thus, while the number of asylum applications in Europe gradually increased from 2005 to 2015, the most dramatic increase was evinced in 2011 (see Figure 6.1).

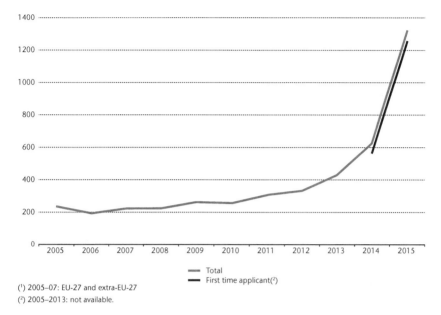

FIGURE 6.1 Asylum Applications (non-EU) in the EU-28 Member States, 2005–15 (thousands)

Source: Eurostat (2016a)

When the first migrant shipwreck occurred near the coast of the Italian island of Lampedusa on October 3, 2013, the focus shifted from managing high numbers of migrants to the tragedy of migrant deaths. Of the 1,664,211 persons who attempted to cross the Mediterranean Sea between 2000 and 2015, some 26,115 lost their life (Fargues 2016: 2). Unsurprisingly, as the number of migrant deaths increased, so did the salience of migration and asylum policy.

Italy, one of the main transit countries in Europe, has been greatly affected by the migrant and refugee crisis. Although it is only ranked as the fourth country in terms of the number of first-time asylum applications among EU member states (see Figure 6.2), its geographic position places it at the center of the Mediterranean migration routes as an entry point into the EU.

As mentioned earlier, Italy's policy for coping with immigration and the refugee crisis has changed over time. In the 1990s, Italy faced its first "refugee crisis" due to large inflows of Albanian refugees fleeing political turmoil. At that time, the Italian government identified a set of priority actions to manage the emergency, including: a) the provision of essential goods delivered directly to the territory of the country of origin; b) the deployment of semi-military and military forces in the prevention of migration; and c) the development of domestic emergency legislation aiming at reinforcing border controls. To deal with the migration emergency, from September 1991 to December 1993, Italy

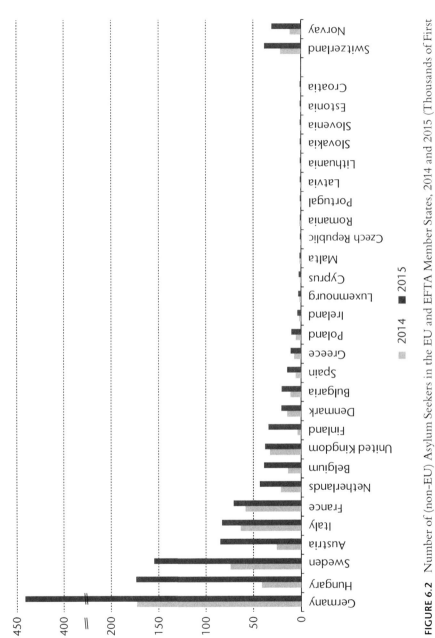

FIGURE 6.2 Number of (non-EU) Asylum Seekers in the EU and EFTA Member States, 2014 and 2015 (Thousands of First Time Applicants)

Source: Eurostat (2016b)

carried out an intervention in Albania, codenamed "Operation Pellicano," with the objective of delivering emergency aid, patrolling ports, and ending refugee flows (Ignazi et al. 2012). Later, in 1995, the Italian government approved a restrictive immigration law (Decree n. 489/95) and launched a patrolling operation that was aimed at curbing irregular entry into the country. However, as the crisis continued, the Italian government persuaded the United Nations in 1997 to provide it with a mandate to lead a multinational force of 6,000 soldiers, and Operation Alba was launched to restore order in Albania. In March 1997 the Italian center-left government declared a "state of emergency" and decided that refugees would be allowed to stay in the country for no more than three months.

Since those early years, migration to Europe has become an even more regular phenomenon (Attinà 2015), and Italy has become the main entry point to Europe from the Middle East, North Africa, and sub-Saharan Africa due to its geographic location. In 2010, this trend turned swiftly into a situation of "systemic crisis" due to the uprisings in North Africa (Figure 6.3).

Specifically, from 2010 to 2011, the number of first-time asylum applications in Italy increased from 10,000 to 40,315 (Eurostat 2016b). Moreover, between January and September 2011, some 42,807 people were recorded as entering Italy illegally by sea, compared to less than 5,000 in 2010, less than 10,000 in 2009, and an annual average of 18,788 in the preceding decade (Fargues and Fandrich 2012: 4). At that time, the Italian approach to migration was similar to the policy adopted during the Albanian crisis and was based on two main pillars: a) reinforcing bilateral cooperation with those African countries that were the points of departure of the smuggling boats, and b) reinforcing the surveillance of the western Mediterranean maritime borders by launching national patrolling operations and requesting EU participation in the protection of the European Union's Mediterranean borders.

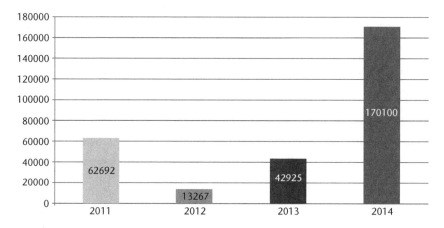

FIGURE 6.3 Trend of Migrant Arrivals in Italy

Source: Migration Policy Centre n.d.

In December 2000, Italy and Libya had already signed a cooperation agreement aimed at tackling irregular immigration, and in 2003, during the Italian presidency of the European Union, the EU launched a joint border patrol operation, the "Neptune Project," composed of border guards from various EU member states to patrol the Strait of Sicily. A common surveillance system located in the Sicilian city of Palermo was established with the aim of preventing and monitoring illegal flows of migrants in the western Mediterranean. Then, in 2004, a unilateral Italian initiative was launched, the "Constant Vigilance Mission," operated by the Italian Navy. The objective of this mission was to control the Strait of Sicily to prevent irregular entry. Then, in 2006/2007 Italy was heavily involved in the "Hermes" and "Nautilus" operations that were launched and coordinated by Frontex, the European Union border and coast guard agency.

In 2008 the Italian center-right government of Prime Minister Silvio Berlusconi signed the "Treaty on Friendship, Partnership, and Cooperation" (known as the Benghazi Treaty) with Libya.[1] Based on that agreement, Italy began to intercept migrant boats in the Mediterranean Sea and to return unidentified passengers to Libya. Even after Qaddafi's defeat, the securitized migration policy persisted. Indeed, after Qaddafi's ouster, Italy reached a new agreement with the National Transitional Council of Libya on June 17, 2011 aimed at cooperating in the fight against illegal immigration, including the return of irregular migrants. The main provisions of that agreement included an increase in patrolling operations along the Libyan coast and the establishment of a satellite detection system for control of Libyan land borders. On the basis of that agreement, Italian coast guard and naval patrols were able to return migrants to Libya without checking to determine whether any of them needed international protection. As a result, over 13,000 migrants were returned in 2011.

On April 5, 2011, Italy also signed an agreement with the Tunisian Government aimed at facilitating the readmission of irregular immigrants and reinforcing police cooperation and control of maritime borders. The Italian government offered €200 million in aid and credit in return for Tunisia's cooperation in preventing further departures as well as accepting returned migrants, a move that led almost immediately to a 75 percent drop in the flow of Tunisian migrants.

In short, from the early 1990s until 2011, the Italian approach to refugees was security-oriented and focused on the physical control of borders as well as on bilateral agreements with African states. This approach was fully consistent with the European Union's immigration policy. What was unclear, however, was whether the repatriations complied with international law and the principle of *non-refoulement*. The Benghazi agreement, in particular, which was abrogated after the fall of the Qaddafi government, was severely criticized by NGOs for its apparent disregard of international legal standards. In 2012, Italy was also condemned by the European Court of Human Rights for violating the prohibition against inhuman or degrading treatment, the prohibition against collective expulsion, and the right to effective remedy, as provided for by the

European Convention for the Protection of Human Rights (European Database of Asylum Law n.d.).

Refugee Crisis: Italian Conditions and European Scenario

The increased pressure of irregular migration flows on Italy can be better analyzed in light of relations between Italy and the European Union. The EU plays the role of "standard setter and norm maker" (Attinà 2016: 20) for the immigration and border policy of its member states. However, even though the EU shares some legislative control with its member states on immigration, it has no power to control its external borders. Instead, member states are charged with the responsibility of acting within a framework of common rules and norms that have developed since the 1990s, with the aim of defining conditions of entry and residency of non-EU nationals. However, since Italy's territory is part of the external and maritime border of the EU, the country plays a key role in the management of EU policy on refugee and immigrations flows. Its immigration policy is also strongly affected by the common standards and norms on migration, asylum, and the management of external borders. As a result, this common system generates external constraints for the Italian management of the refugee crisis.

The first constraint is the result of the Dublin system, which has established criteria and mechanisms for determining which European Union state is responsible for receiving and processing asylum applications submitted by third country nationals.[2] According to the Dublin Regulation, the first state through which an asylum seeker enters the European Union is responsible for receiving and processing the application. Moreover, asylum seekers are obligated to apply for asylum in the first EU country they enter, and duplicate asylum claims in more than one member state by the same person are not permitted. The main aim of the Dublin System is to avoid "asylum shopping" (Guiraudon 2000, 2001), the submission of duplicate claims for asylum in more than one member state by the same person, and "refugees in orbit"—that is, asylum seekers who are unable to find a member state willing to accept their application.

The Dublin system has been strongly criticized as being ineffective and unfair to both asylum seekers as well as to certain member states. One criticism is that its rules increase pressure on the external border regions of the EU, creating serious imbalances in the distribution of applicants. Still others contend that Dublin does not comply with the principle of fair treatment since the European Union has not yet developed harmonized standards in substantive and procedural areas of asylum among its member states.[3] Lastly, many contend that the system does not contain any mechanism for an equitable and balanced distribution of refugees after their asylum claims have been accepted.

Italy faces a major burden as a result of the Dublin Regulation. In addition to the requirement that it must receive and process applications as described previously, it must also conduct background checks on applicants. According to Directive 2008/115/CE, for example, national border authorities of member states are solely responsible for the external border checks of individuals as well as for every decision taken to return irregular third country nationals to their country of origin. As such, Italian border authorities must comply with the common rules since, in the Schengen area, external border controls are intended to compensate for the abolition of internal border checks and must contribute to "the fight against terrorism, illegal immigration networks and the traffic in human beings" (European Council 2001).

The final constraint on the Italian system comes from the Common European Asylum System (CEAS) that was adopted in 1999 to harmonize minimum standards for asylum throughout the EU. Its main provisions were codified by four directives and a regulation. The directives establish a list of minimum standards for a) the temporary protection of displaced persons in the context of a mass influx of people seeking protection (Council of the European Union 2001, 2003);[4] b) the reception of asylum seekers by member states (Council of the European Union 2003);[5] c) the qualifications that third country nationals or stateless persons need to fulfill in order to qualify for international protection and the content of the protection granted (Council of the European Union 2004);[6] and d) the procedural standards in member states for granting and withdrawing refugee status (Council of the European Union 2005).

Between them, the Dublin system and the procedural requirements from the Common European Asylum System increase pressures on Italy's border management in cases of massive inflows of migrants. Moreover, "security concerns" coming from the Schengen system frame Italian policy into a binding set of rules on management and control of the European external borders, which are considered part of European security policy (Geddes 2000; Longo 2016; Mitsilegas 2010; Takle 2012). Since 2013, increasing political instability in some states in the Mediterranean and Middle East turned massive maritime arrivals from "emergency events" to a regular trend. The deaths of thousands of migrants who were trying to enter the EU by sea were a key catalyst of the EU migration and border control regime crisis.

Tragedy in Lampedusa: A Turning Point

On October 3, 2013, more than 300 migrants died in a shipwreck near the Italian island of Lampedusa. It was not the first migrant tragedy in the Mediterranean, but the number of victims (800, as reported by the United Nations) magnetized media attention and shocked public opinion. As a result, on October 18 the Italian government launched the naval operation "Mare Nostrum." Defined as "a military and humanitarian operation aimed at tackling the humanitarian emergency in the Strait of Sicily" with the two-fold purpose of "safeguarding human life at sea, and bringing to justice human traffickers and migrant smugglers" (Italian

Defense Ministry 2016), the operation marked a significant modification in Italian immigration strategy (Attinà 2015), pushing Italy to recognize the humanitarian dimension of immigration policy. The launch of "Mare Nostrum" was the starting point of a new strategy based on a new approach that re-considered immigration policy in light of humanitarian intervention. Operation Mare Nostrum established a complex mechanism of interoperability among Italian military forces, law enforcement agencies, and the Italian Red Cross. Moreover, it was assisted by non-governmental organizations that provided medical and psychological assistance directly to migrants. In a departure from past policies, Mare Nostrum fully complied with international standards concerning the protection of human rights, the protection of migrants, asylum seekers, and refugees, and rescue at sea operations, as established by international humanitarian law and the United Nations (Attinà 2015). Importantly, during the time of its operation, Mare Nostrum contributed to the rescue of around 150,000 refuges—among whom 12,000 were unaccompanied minors—and to the arrest of 728 traffickers of migrants.[7]

Not surprisingly, Mare Nostrum was welcomed by non-governmental organizations and by the UNHCR, but it was criticized by many EU member states amid fears that it was encouraging smugglers and migrants to undertake more trips to Europe. However, it broke the prevailing perception of immigration as a security concern, initiating debate on the need for collective responses to sea rescue missions, safer methods for refugees to seek asylum, and for greater sharing of the burden among EU member states. However, despite the fact that financial constraints forced the Italian government to end Mare Nostrum only one year after its launch, Italy has continued to promote a change of EU immigration policy since that time (Panebianco 2016). To this end, Italy promotes the need to include a humanitarian approach and rescue activities in border control practices, as well as the need to establish a common policy on migration—one based on a genuine burden-sharing system (Renzi 2015).

In place of Mare Nostrum, on November 1, 2014, the EU launched "Triton," a search and rescue operation that provided additional technical equipment and border guards to Italy. Presented as replacing Mare Nostrum, Triton was attributed to the (rotating) Italian Presidency of the European Council. Triton differed significantly from previous Italian operations, such as Mare Nostrum. First, it was focused more on border control than on humanitarian action: its main aim was "to implement coordinated operational activities at the external sea borders of the Central Mediterranean region in order to control irregular migration flows towards the territory of the Member States of the European Union and to tackle cross-border crime" (Frontex 2014). Second, its activities of search-and-rescue in the Western Mediterranean had a range of no more than 30 miles from the coast, while Mare Nostrum had a range of 120 miles. Not as effective, Triton failed to prevent the most dramatic shipwreck that had ever occurred in the Mediterranean, one that took place in April 2015 when almost 1,000 people died in a shipwreck 60 miles off the Libyan coast.

As a result of this disaster, Italy organized rescue operations and called once again for a common humanitarian approach. European institutions reacted by turning the political debate away from the "fight against illegal immigration" to one of "refugee issues" (Panebianco 2016: 14). However, the political decisions that followed did not fundamentally alter the EU's security approach to migration. As the number of shipwrecks in the Sicilian Channel continued to increase during 2015, the migration crisis remained at the top of the EU agenda. Again, Italy tried to frame common EU action with an approach based on humanitarianism, burden-sharing, and solidarity among member states. Soon thereafter, the European Commission adopted the European Agenda on Migration, a non-binding political program that included some of the Italian positions, with short-term priorities that included actions to prevent further loss of migrant lives at sea by providing joint search and rescue operations, the safe and legal resettlement of people in Europe, regional protection, as well as development programs and aid to the most affected member states located along the EU's external borders. Moreover, the European Agenda on Migration also provided a system of support for member states to help them identify, register, and fingerprint migrants.

It is important to note, however, that the few actions taken by the European Union following the adoption of the European Agenda on Migration were not consistent with the agenda's premise. For example, in July and September 2015, the Justice and Home Affairs Council adopted a "relocation system" aimed at burden-sharing among European partners. The plan envisioned a transfer of 160,000 asylum seekers from Italy and Greece,[8] the two principal member states where refugees arrive and are identified, to other member states, where their asylum applications are to be processed and where, if successful, they will be granted the right to live. This measure, intended to apply the principle of solidarity in refugee management, did not achieve this goal and, furthermore, does not comply with Italian requests. Specifically, it is a provisional emergency mechanism that does not establish a structural policy of burden-sharing on asylum seekers. The program also does not alleviate the workload of Italy and Greece in terms of rescue activity and identification procedures. Furthermore, the Council decided to recognize the possibility that member states could declare a temporary inability to comply with the relocation operations. Moreover, the Council's decision established that relocations should take place over two years, but it did not define a mandatory timetable, instead allowing each member state to develop its own schedule for such transfers. According to Article 5 of the decision, member states should indicate at least once every three months the number of applicants to be relocated to their territory by submitting a formal pledge to the Commission. Based on the information on the number of pledges, Italy and Greece are asked to identify the individual applicants who will be relocated to the other Member States, giving priority to vulnerable people. The receiving Member State of relocation may decide not to approve the relocation of an applicant only if there are reasonable grounds for regarding him or her as a danger to their national security or public.

Conclusion

This article has analyzed the Italian management of the refugee crisis through the lens of two competing arguments: a security and a humanitarian approach. The analysis of decisions and actions taken by Italian governments since the first serious refugee crisis in the mid-1990s has revealed two distinct approaches. The first approach, connected with the securitization of migration, produced policies that were intended to decrease arrivals to Italy by increasing border controls, pushing back irregular migrants, and reinforcing bilateral cooperation with third countries, all in an effort to curb irregular flows of migrants. Defined as a "conventional response" (Attinà 2016: 25), this security approach was in line with then-EU policy on migration, strongly anchored in the principle of closed borders. However, in 2013, the launch of Mare Nostrum turned the Italian approach from a security-based to a humanitarian approach. The increasing number of shipwrecks and deaths at sea, as well as the burden derived from being a country on the forefront of the refugee crisis attempting to manage the western Mediterranean flows, challenged the security approach. Mare Nostrum represented the first steps towards a new humanitarian approach aimed at conducting search and rescue operations at sea and establishing safe corridors for the entry of asylum seekers. Even though this new Italian approach was not fully accepted by the EU, it nevertheless opened a fissure in Europe's system of closed borders. As we have argued above, the European Agenda for Migration adopted a number of the Italian positions and became a starting point for a revised EU common policy on migration and refugees (European Commission 2015). Starting from the assumption that search and rescue efforts should be increased to restore the level of intervention provided under Mare Nostrum, the European Agenda for Migration recognized for the first time the complex nature of migratory flows and the need to adopt humanitarian actions in order to save human lives at sea. Moreover, assistance for frontline states was placed on the political agenda for the first time.

In April 2016, at a meeting of EU foreign affairs ministers, Italy presented a non-paper titled "Migration Compact: Contribution to an EU Strategy for External Action on Migration" (Italian Ministry of Foreign Affairs 2016). This document further sets forth that "migration may represent an opportunity both for the EU and partner countries, in terms of economic growth and development, and for an aging Europe in terms of sustainability of social security systems." It calls for the development of common policies that encourage the legal entry of third country nationals into the European Union and for a system of genuine solidarity among member states, with a particular regard to emergency situations. Special attention is focused on a proposal to create economic and financial instruments aimed at linking development of African countries to EU migration policy. The main instruments proposed for this are the "EU-Africa bonds"—financial instruments aimed at facilitating the access of African countries to capital markets, and other innovative financing initiatives (for example, facilitating remittances and their re-investment and blending mechanisms, among others), in cooperation with international financial organizations. Moreover, Italy's Migration Compact confirms the Italian position on the need to establish legal migration opportunities and resettlement schemes as compensation to those countries that establish national asylum systems in line with international standards. However, although several measures approved for the implementation of the European Commission Agenda on Migration partially adopted the Italian approach, Italy's proposed Migration Compact is not at the top of the EU's migration agenda. This notwithstanding, there is room for optimism. The EU has begun to alter its approach to migration. It has recognized the relevance of humanitarian intervention and introduced the topic of solidarity into the management of migration and asylum policy. This new approach has challenged the old security approach to migration and has created certain fissures in the wall of the EU's closed borders policy. Thus, an important challenge for Italy today is to play a leading role in this debate so as to change, not only the common narrative, but also the common policy measures to be adopted by Europe.

Notes

1 The text of the Treaty is annexed to the Italian Ratification Law, n. 7, February 6, 2009.
2 In January 2014 the third version of the Dublin Regulation entered into force. Even if the Schengen Code is fully incorporated into the body of rules governing the EU, it does not encompass all 28 Member States. Bulgaria, Croatia, Cyprus, Ireland, Romania, and the United Kingdom are not part of the Schengen system. However, Bulgaria and Romania are currently in the process of joining it. In addition, the following non-EU States have joined the Schengen area: Iceland, Norway, Switzerland, and Liechtenstein. See European Union (2013b).
3 European Commission, COM (2008) 820 def.2008/0243 (COD).
4 The 2003 Directive was revised in 2013 by Directive 2013/33/EU. See European Union (2013a).
5 Revised in 2013 by Directive 2013/33/EU.
6 Revised in 2011 by Directive 2011/95/EU. See European Union (2011).
7 Figures are taken from Italian Parliament, DOC. XVI-BIS N. 3, 2014.
8 In July the Council agreed to relocate 40,000 asylum seekers. See Council of the European Union (2015a). In September it agreed on the relocation of an additional 120,000 asylum seekers. See Council of the European Union (2015b).

References

Attinà, Fulvio. 2015. "Europe Faces the Immigration Crisis: Perceptions and Scenarios." *ReShape Online Papers Series*. Catania: University of Catania. Retrieved August 2, 2016 (www.dsps.unict.it/sites/default/files/files/repaper10(1).pdf).

Attinà, Fulvio. 2016. "Migration Drivers, the E.U. External Migration Policy and Crisis Management." *Romanian Journal of European Affairs* 16(4):15–31.

Buzan, Barry, Ole Waever, and Jaap de Wilde. 1998. *A New Security Framework for Analysis.* Boulder and London: Lynne Rienner.

Council of the European Union. 2001. "Council Directive 2001/55/Ec of 20 July 2001 on Minimum Standards for Giving Temporary Protection in the Event of a Mass Influx of Displaced Persons and on Measures Promoting a Balance of Efforts between Member States in Receiving Such Persons and Bearing the Consequences Thereof." *Official Journal of the European Communities* L 212/12. Retreived September 2, 2015 (http://eur-lex.europa.eu/legal-content/en/TXT/?uri=CELEX:32001L0055).

Council of the European Union. 2003. "Council Directive 2003/9/Ec of 27 January 2003 Laying Down Minimum Standards for the Reception of Asylum Seekers." *Official Journal of the European Union* L 31/18. Retreived July 3, 2016. (http://eur-lex.europa.eu/legalcontent/GA/TXT/?uri=OJ:L:2003:031:TOC).

Council of the European Union. 2004. "Council Directive 2004/83/Ec of 29 April 2004 on Minimum Standards for the Qualification and Status of Third Country Nationals or Stateless Persons as Refugees or as Persons Who Otherwise Need International Protection and the Content of the Protection Granted." *Official Journal of the European Union* L 304/12. Retreived July 3, 2016. (http://eur-lex.europa.eu/LexUriServ/LexUriServ.do?uri=CELEX:32004L0083:en:HTML).

Council of the European Union. 2005. "Council Directive 2005/85/Ec of 1 December 2005 on Minimum Standards on Procedures in Member States for Granting and Withdrawing Refugee Status." *Official Journal of the European Union* L 326/13. Retreived July 3, 2016 (http://eur-lex.europa.eu/legal-content/EN/ALL/?uri=CELEX%3A32005L0085).

Council of the European Union. 2015a. "Resolution of the Representatives of the Governments of the Member States Meeting within the Council on Relocating from Greece and Italy 40 000 Persons in Clear Need of International Protection." 11131/15. Retreived September 15, 2016 (http://data.consilium.europa.eu/doc/document/ST-11131-2015-INIT/en/pdf).

Council of the European Union. 2015b. "Council Decision Establishing Provisional Measures in the Area of International Protection for the Benefit of Italy and Greece." 12098/15. Retreived September 15, 2016 (http://data.consilium.europa.eu/doc/document/ST-12098-2015-INIT/en/pdf).

European Commission. 2015. "A European Agenda on Migration: Communication from the Commission to the European Parliament, the Council, the European Economic and Social Committee and the Committee of the Regions, Com(2015) 240." May 13. Retrieved February 23, 2017 (http://ec.europa.eu/dgs/home-affairs/what-we-do/policies/european-agenda-migration/index_en.htm).

European Council. 2001. "Presidency Conclusions: Laeken December 14 and 15." Retrieved February 17, 2017. (www.consilium.europa.eu/uedocs/cms_data/docs/pressdata/en/ec/68827.pdf).

European Database of Asylum Law. n.d. "ECTHR: Hirsi Jamaa and Others V Italy [Gc], Application No. 27765/09." Brussels: European Database of Asylum Law. Retrieved February 19, 2017. (www.asylumlawdatabase.eu/en/content/ecthr-hirsi-jamaa-and-others-v-italy-gc-application-no-2776509).

European Union. 2011. "Directive 2011/95/Eu of the European Parliament and of the Council of 13 December 2011 on Standards for the Qualification of Third-Country Nationals or Stateless Persons as Beneficiaries of International Protection, for a Uniform Status for Refugees or for Persons Eligible for Subsidiary Protection, and for the

Content of the Protection Granted (Recast)." *Official Journal of the European Union* L 337/9. Retreived September 15, 2016 (http://eur-lex.europa.eu/legal-content/en/TXT/?uri=celex%3A32011L0095).

European Union. 2013a. "Directive 2013/33/Eu of the European Parliament and of the Council of 26 June 2013 Laying Down Standards for the Reception of Applicants for International Protection." *Official Journal of the European Union* L 180/96. Retreived March 16, 2017 (http://eur-lex.europa.eu/legal-content/EN/TXT/?uri=celex%3A32013L0033).

European Union. 2013b. "Regulation (Eu) No 604/2013 of the European Parliament and of the Council Establishing the Criteria and Mechanisms for Determining the Member State Responsible for Examining an Application for International Protection Lodged in One of the Member States by a Third-Country National or a Stateless Person (Recast)." *Official Journal of the European Union* L 180/31. Retreived March 16, 2017 (http://eur-lex.europa.eu/legal-content/en/ALL/?uri=celex%3A32013R0604).

Eurostat. 2016a. "Asylum Statistics." Retrieved February 19, 2017 (http://ec.europa.eu/eurostat/statistics-explained/index.php/Asylum_statistics).

Eurostat. 2016b. "Asylum and First Time Asylum Applicants: Annual Aggregated Data." Retrieved February 26, 2017 (http://ec.europa.eu/eurostat/tgm/table.do?tab=table&init=1&language=en&pcode=tps00191&plugin=1).

Fargues, Philippe. 2016. "Who Are the Million Migrants Who Entered Europe without a Visa in 2015?" *Population and Societies* 532:1–4.

Fargues, Philippe and Christine Fandrich. 2012. "Migration after the Arab Spring: Research Report 2012/2009." Florence: European University Institute.

Frontex. 2014. "Archive of Operations: E.P.N. Triton." Retrieved February 19, 2017 (http://frontex.europa.eu/operations/archive-of-operations/NkKUdU).

Geddes, Andrew. 2000. *Immigration and European Integration, towards Fortress Europe?* Manchester: Manchester University Press.

Guiraudon, Virginie. 2000. "European Integration and Migration Policy: Vertical Policy-Making as Venue Shopping." *Journal of Common Market Studies* 38(2):251–71.

Guiraudon, Virgine. 2001. "De-Nationalizing Control: Analyzing State Responses to Constraints on Migration Control." Pp. 31–64 in Virgine Guiraudon and Christian Joppke, eds. *Controlling a New Migration World*. London: Routledge.

Huysmans, Jef and Vicki Squire. 2009. "Migration and Security." Pp. 169–79 in Victor Mauer and Myriam Dunn Cavelty, eds. *The Routledge Handbook of Security Studies*. London: Routledge.

Ignazi, Piero, Giampiero Giacomello, and Fabrizio Coticchio. 2012. *Italy's Military Operations Abroad: Just Don't Call It War!* Basingstoke, UK: Palgrave Macmillan.

Italian Defense Ministry. 2016. "Mare Nostrum Operation." Rome: Italian Defense Ministry. Retrieved February 19, 2017 (www.marina.difesa.it/EN/operations/Pagine/MareNostrum.aspx).

Italian Ministry of Foreign Affairs. 2016. "Migration Compact: Contribution to an E.U. Strategy for External Action on Migration." Rome: Italian Ministry of Foreign Affairs. Retrieved February 19, 2017 (www.governo.it/sites/governo.it/files/immigrazione_0.pdf).

Longo, Francesca. 2016. "La Politica Di Migrazione Nell'unione Europea Tra Vecchie E Nuove Sfide. [The European Union's Migration Policy between Old and New Challenges]." Pp. 47–69 in Stefania Panebianco, ed. *Sulle Onde Del Mediterraneo*. Milan: Egea.

Mascia, Marco. 2011. "Human Security between Conceptualisation and Practical Enactment: The United Nations and European Union Vision." *Pace Diritti Umani* 2:7–26.

Migration Policy Centre. n.d. "Refugees." Migration Policy Centre, European Policy Initiative. Robert Schuman Centre for Advanced Studies. Retrieved February 19, 2017 (www.migrationpolicycentre.eu/migrant-crisis/migrant-crisis-refugees/).

Mitsilegas, Valsamis. 2010. "Extraterritorial Immigration Control in the 21st Century: The Individual and the State Transformed." Pp. 39–69 in Valsamis Mitsilegas and Bernard Ryan, eds. *Extraterritorial Immigration Control: Legal Challenges*. Leiden: Martinus Nijhoff.

Panebianco, Stefania. 2016. "The Mare Nostrum Operation and the Sar Approach: The Italian Response to Address the Mediterranean Migration Crisis." *EUMedEA Online Working Paper Series*. University of Catania. Retrieved March 16, 2016 (www.dsps.unict.it/sites/default/files/files/panbianco_EUMedEA_JMWP_03_2016__.pdf).

Renzi, Matteo. 2015. "The Mediterranean Migrant Emergency Is Not Italy's: It Is Europe's." *The Guardian*. Retreived March 16, 2017 (www.theguardian.com/commentisfree/2015/jun/23/mediterranean-migrant-crisis-not-italy-but-europe).

Takle, Marianne. 2012. "The Treaty of Lisbon and the European Border Control Regime." *Journal of Contemporary European Research* 8(3):280–99.

Vietti, Francesca and Todd Scribner. 2013. "Human Insecurity: Understanding International Migration from a Human Security Perspective." *Journal of Migration and Human Security* 1(1):17–31.

7

CHALLENGED INTEGRATION

Europe's Refugee Crisis

Danijela Dudley

SAN JOSE STATE UNIVERSITY

> *Why is the European Union, an organization with professed goals of promoting peace and economic prosperity while championing the ideals of tolerance and human rights, unable to respond adequately to a humanitarian crisis within its borders? While the EU has faced severe criticism for its inadequate response to the crisis, this chapter argues that the response is consistent with the EU's current institutional structure, deliberately hesitant in its integration efforts. Fast enlargement to the east led to the inclusion of countries with varying levels of commitment to the ideals of tolerance and human rights. As a result, while economic policies have been entirely integrated and transferred to the EU's competency, more divisive issues, such as asylum and immigration policies, have faced slower integration and institutionalization. Accordingly, the hesitancy in institutionalization of asylum and immigration policy resulted in a failure of the European Union to act with a unified voice. Instead, the refugee crisis produced a number of ad hoc responses from individual member states, leading to an emergence of chain-link fences along the EU's edges and reintroduction of borders within it.*

For decades, a borderless Europe has been hailed as an unprecedented accomplishment dedicated to achieving peace and economic prosperity while championing the ideals of tolerance and human rights. This ambitious project of unifying European states into "an area without internal frontiers" has been in the making for over six decades. It has, surprisingly, been able to withstand many internal and external challenges, such as the collapse of the Soviet Union in its immediate neighborhood, the bloody civil war in former Yugoslavia, the reunification of Germany, the 2008 global financial crisis, and the recent United Kingdom referendum on leaving the European Union. These challenges notwithstanding, the EU's core principles seemed robust and resilient. However, the recent sudden surge in the number of asylum seekers from the Middle East and North Africa has starkly revealed the weakness of the EU's Common Asylum Policy and challenged its professed commitment to tolerance and the protection of human rights.

The refugee crisis produced two related challenges for the EU. First, since all EU member states are parties to the 1951 Convention Relating to the Status of Refugees and its Protocol (the Geneva Convention), they are obligated to offer protection to those who have a reasonable fear of danger on the basis of race, religion, nationality, or political opinion (United Nations 1951, 1967). Different member states of the EU, however, have demonstrated varying levels of commitment to fulfilling their responsibilities under international law.

In addition to revealing many member states' unwillingness to realize their international obligations, the sudden influx of asylum seekers also challenged the organization's internal cohesion. The inability of the EU to act with a unified voice resulted in a number of *ad hoc* responses from individual member states. As a result, the EU's ability to weather crises in which member states' core values are challenged was called into question. Thus, unlike situations faced by the EU in the past, the refugee crisis saw the emergence of chain-link fences along its external borders and the re-introduction of internal border controls, thereby violating one of the main principles of the European project—the free movement of people.

While the EU has been subject to many criticisms for its slow and inconsistent response to the refugee crisis (see Popescu 2016; Roberts et al. 2016; Selanec 2015), this article argues that its response reflects the European Union's current state of incomplete integration. As an experiment in international integration, the EU has yet to reach the level of cohesion that characterizes sovereign states. Thus, while the level of integration has progressively been increasing and more policy areas have been moved to EU jurisdiction, the organization's evolution has been characterized by the slow and incomplete integration of those policy areas that affect member states' external security and cultural values.

Ultimately an economic organization, the EU ensured the economic and, to some extent, political cooperation of new member states by including a range of detailed economic and political criteria in their pre-accession negotiations, such as the free movement of goods, taxation policies, intellectual property rights, consumer and health protection, and similar. At the same time, the more contentious issues of foreign, security, and defense policy, as well as immigration and asylum, were only partly negotiated within the broad framework and were to be mostly coordinated after accession. As I illustrate below, the absence of institutionalized central authority to coordinate the EU's response to the refugee crisis propelled individual member states to design their own independent responses to the crisis.

The first section of this article introduces the slow and incomplete development of European Union asylum policy. Next, the article assesses the EU's response to the crisis and observes that the delays in its response were brought about by the absence of institutionalized authority as a result of incomplete integration. Since the regulation of national asylum policies was only partially established at the supranational level, member states were expected to manage the crisis independently, while adhering to the common framework that had been established by the EU. Indeed, even when the EU attempted concerted action, it strove to reach a consensus among member states, delaying its response even further. Thus, the third section of the article analyzes the consequences of the absence of central authority, illustrating how member states' individual responses to the crisis diverged sharply. In the concluding section, the article assesses the implications of the refugee crisis for the future of the European Union.

Development of Europe's Asylum Policy

Asylum policy is a relatively new item on the EU agenda, emerging out of the practical need to grapple with the absence of internal borders, as the establishment of a truly borderless single market called for some level of harmonization of immigration and asylum policies as a necessary step for a region that guarantees free movement throughout its territory. Until the late 1990s, however, visa, asylum, and immigration policies were part of the "third pillar," allowing states to have almost unrestricted sovereignty in this policy area, and giving EU institutions very little authority over these issues.[1] Regulation at the EU level mostly had the effect of *urging* member states to comply with certain procedures to harmonize their visa and asylum policies. This hesitant transfer of jurisdiction to the EU was, of course, in line with the organization's pattern of slow integration in policy areas that challenge security and cultural values. Namely, while economic integration was completed with all deliberate speed, political integration occurred at a slower pace. Foreign and security policy, however, have yet to be integrated.

As one of the more divisive issues, asylum and immigration policy has only recently been transferred to the first pillar and, subsequently, only partially institutionalized at the supranational level. One of the earliest attempts to regulate certain aspects of immigration and asylum policy took place in the early 1990s. Although asylum policy at the time was still subject to intergovernmental decision-making, the EU produced the Dublin Regulation which specified that all asylum seekers within the EU would be processed in, and assessed by, the country through which they first enter the Union (European Union 1990).[2] Intended to ensure order, the Dublin system was designed to help the EU keep track of individuals who have entered its territory and are receiving international protection.

Further changes to asylum policy occurred in the late 1990s with the entry into force of the Treaty of Amsterdam, which partly transferred visa, asylum, and immigration policies to the first pillar, making them subject to ordinary legislative procedure and community decision-making processes (European Union 1997). Accordingly, the Commission was empowered to make proposals on asylum regulation, while the Council and the Parliament could make decisions without achieving member state unanimity.[3] Then, at a European Council meeting in Tampere in 1999, EU leaders set the stage for the creation of a common EU asylum policy by agreeing to work "towards establishing a Common European Asylum System, based on the full and inclusive application of the Geneva Convention, thus ensuring that nobody is sent back to persecution, i.e. maintaining the principle of non-refoulement" (European Council 1999: sec. 2.13).

The move of immigration policies to the area governed by the ordinary legislative procedure and the European Council's call for a Common European Asylum System (CEAS) provided the EU the authority to initiate reform of the system by creating a set of unified rules. The Amsterdam and Tampere decisions were subsequently followed by a number of decisions and directives outlining the rights of refugees and the responsibilities of member states.[4] For example, a 2004 Qualifications Directive established common criteria for granting asylum in line with obligations under the Geneva Convention and guaranteed a set of rights for the beneficiaries of international protection, such as the right to obtain residence permits and valid travel documents, as well as the right to employment, education, social welfare, and health care (Council of the European Union 2004). This directive was replaced with an even more rigorous one in 2011, giving those in need of international protection additional benefits and assigning even greater responsibilities to the states processing applications (European Union 2011).

It is important to note that, while both directives were intended to standardize the processes by which qualifications for asylum were determined and sought to provide equal consideration to applicants no matter where they submitted their application within the EU, the directives, in fact, increased the likelihood that states' policies would diverge. That is, while any country could be the first entry point for asylum seekers in principle, the reality was (and is) that visa requirements, tight airport security, and financial restrictions usually prevent refugees from arriving to the EU by plane. Thus, the vast majority of asylum seekers enter the EU through its external land borders. The effect of this was that the Dublin Regulations established countries' geographic location as the main determinant of the responsibilities they would assume in managing the influx of refugees. This placed a disproportionate burden on countries located on the outer edges of the EU, which became particularly problematic when large numbers of asylum seekers started utilizing the Western Balkans route, overwhelming Hungary and Greece with thousands of people arriving at their borders.

The pressures were further exacerbated by states' perceptions and fears about the future consequences of existing regulations. Specifically, according to the Dublin Regulations, a person who has been granted protection under international law can obtain permanent residence in a state other than the one that granted the protection after s/he has established permanent residency in the original state, a process which takes five years (Council of the European Union 2011). Thus, peripheral states concluded that they would not only have to process all the applications, but they would also be bound to host the asylum recipients, providing them with such EU-guaranteed rights as employment, education, social welfare, and health care for at least five years. These calculations likely compounded the states' unwillingness to fulfill their duties as asylum-processing states.

In addition to the aforementioned regulations—which were designed to accommodate routine occurrences of asylum seekers—the EU had taken into account the possibility of a mass influx of refugees in the 2001 Directive on Temporary Protection (Council of the European Union 2001). With the goal of promoting a "balance of effort between Member States in receiving and bearing the consequences of receiving [refugees]" (Art. 1), the Directive established that, "for the duration of the temporary protection, the Member States shall cooperate with each other with regard to transferral of the residence of persons enjoying temporary protection from one Member State to another, subject to the consent of the persons concerned to such transferral" (Art. 26). As the directive implies, the activation of this temporary protection scheme would allow member states to share the burden of a sudden influx of asylum seekers. However, the implementation of the directive depended on the consent of both the state receiving the overflow of refugees and well as of the asylum applicants themselves. As such, it never went into effect.

The second and perhaps more significant option was only later presented by Article 78(3) of the Treaty on the Functioning of the European Union (TFEU) (European Union 2012), which established that

> in the event of one or more Member States being confronted with an emergency situation characterized by a sudden inflow of nationals of third countries, the Council, on a proposal from the Commission, may adopt provisional measures for the benefit of the Member State(s) concerned. It shall act after consulting the European Parliament (European Union 2012).[5]

The activation of Article 78(3) TFEU would provide an exception to the Dublin Regulations to alleviate pressures on the peripheral countries by allowing other states to absorb some of the responsibilities in processing applications. Since this was the only legal provision that granted the EU institutions authority to act in regards to the refugee crisis, it was the one the EU ultimately invoked in an effort to find a solution to the deteriorating refugee situation.

The European Union Response to the Refugee Crisis

The 2001 Temporary Protection Mechanism, participation in which would have been voluntary, was never activated. Instead, the situation on the ground deteriorated as member countries were torn between waiting for a solution from the EU or improvising their own responses. Although the Arab Spring brought large numbers of refugees to the European Union as early as 2011 (mostly via the Mediterranean and Aegean Seas), the sudden increase in the number of asylum seekers that occurred in 2015 appears to have taken everyone by surprise. During that year, the EU was faced with over 1.3 million asylum seekers, an increase of 700,000 over the previous year (Eurostat 2016). This influx created a heavy burden on Italy, Greece, and Hungary, which were the main entry points for those arriving from the Middle East and North Africa. It is important to note that these three countries were not only faced with a mass movement of people, but, in line with EU regulations, were also expected to process asylum applications of all those crossing their borders.

Initially, the politically sensitive nature of immigration and asylum issues led the EU to respond by focusing its efforts on preventing individuals from reaching its territory through better policing of borders and combating trafficking and illegal immigration. Far less attention was devoted to devising crisis management strategies to deal with the internal EU situation. As a result, the EU attempted to prevent refugees from reaching its territory, but those who did make it were left as the responsibility of the peripheral states to process in line with existing regulations.

One of the earliest calls for addressing the *internal* crisis came from the European Council in an April 2015 special session held in response to a number of tragedies suffered by asylum seekers while crossing the Mediterranean and the Aegean Seas. The session called for a "rapid and full transposition and effective implementation of the Common European Asylum System by all participating Member States." It also called for the development of a "more systemic and *geographically comprehensive approach to migration*" (European Council 2015, emphasis added). This call was the result of leaders' realization that the crisis inside the European Union had deteriorated, as the EU experienced nearly 210,000 asylum applications during the first three months of 2015, marking a 74 percent increase compared to the same period in 2014 (European Asylum Support Office 2015).[6]

For its part, the European Parliament attempted to provide a more structured response, calling for the establishment of binding quotas for the relocation of refugees among member states and by shaming those countries that had refused to share the burden of hosting asylum seekers (European Parliament 2015). Specifically, the resolution urged "the Member States to make greater contributions to existing resettlement programs, *especially those Member States which have not contributed anything*" (European Parliament 2015: Art. 8, emphasis added). This resolution was followed by another important step when the European Commission published the European Agenda on Migration in which it recognized the need for a consistent set of policies across the EU, as well as for more coordinated action among EU institutions, member states, and international organizations in dealing with the crisis:

> We need to restore confidence in our ability to bring together European and national efforts to address migration, to meet our international and

ethical obligations and to work together in an effective way, in accordance with the principles of solidarity and shared responsibility. No Member State can effectively address migration alone. It is clear that we need a new, more European approach. This requires using all policies and tools at our disposal—combining internal and external policies to best effect (European Commission 2015c: 2).

The Commission also pledged to undertake further steps which would involve establishing a strict distribution scheme to "ensure a fair and balanced participation of all Member States to this common effort" (European Commission 2015c: 4). The distribution scheme would be based on such criteria as GDP, size of population, unemployment rate, and past numbers of asylum seekers accepted. It also proposed to trigger the emergency response system envisioned under Article 78(3) TFEU.

Interestingly, while the Commission did follow through with a relocation scheme of 40,000 and the resettlement of 20,000 individuals,[7] it simultaneously inhibited a swift decision by requesting that the Council reach a consensus on the proposed scheme. As a result, the divisive nature of the issue delayed finalization of the agreement. Although, in the end, the decision to relocate 40,000 individuals from Italy and Greece over the next two years was reached unanimously (Council of the European Union 2015a), by the point that decision was reached, the European Union was experiencing a massive increase in the number of asylum applicants. By July 2015, the number of applications surpassed 100,000 for the first time, while that number reached nearly 150,000 in August (European Asylum Support Office 2016), making the Council's decision to relocate 40,000 individuals, albeit a unanimous one, rather insignificant and unlikely to make any significant improvement to the situation.

While the Council was still debating the proposal to relocate 40,000 individuals, the Commission put forward an even more ambitious proposal for the relocation of an additional 120,000 individuals from Italy, Greece, and Hungary over the next two years (European Commission 2015e). Faced with the dilemma of maintaining unity among member states by striving for a consensus or making a decision on the Commission's proposal, the Council opted for expediency, likely motivated by the fact that in September alone over 170,000 individuals sought asylum in the EU (European Asylum Support Office 2016). While the Council reached a decision in less than two weeks (Council of the European Union 2015b), the decision revealed deep-seated divergence in attitudes among EU member states.

Divided Union

In spite of the obstacles in reaching an agreement, the two decisions on relocating 160,000 asylum seekers appeared to signal an encouraging development toward collective crisis management. According to Jean Asselborn, Luxembourg's Minister for Immigration and Asylum, who chaired the Council, the decision, although divided, was far superior to any alternatives. Without this decision, "Europe would otherwise have been more divided and its credibility damaged. . . . I will leave you to imagine the divisions that would have arisen, if we had failed to reach an agreement" (Presidency of the Council 2015). Despite the willingness of many member states to work toward a common solution, unfortunately their decision was overshadowed by objections from certain East European member states as well as the subsequent inconsistent implementation of that decision.

Specifically, the relocation decision was taken using a qualified majority vote, passing over the objections of the Czech Republic, Hungary, Romania, and Slovakia, which refused to support the proposal. According to Hungary's Prime Minister Victor Orban, "We have to defend Hungary and Europe, the borders of the country and our way of life, our culture and sovereignty" (quoted in Troianovski et al. 2015). This objection was consistent with the East European member states' opposition to EU asylum practices. Before joining the EU, democratization efforts in many East European states had been shaped significantly by their desire for international integration, and the EU had provided the necessary impetus for the advancement of democracy in the region since membership in the club of European states is conditional on a democratic form of government, respect for human rights, and the rule of law. However, while new entrants adopted the legislation necessary for membership and became functioning democracies by pledging a commitment to the same principles of freedom, democracy, and respect for human rights enshrined in the Treaty on European Union, they appeared to maintain core values (especially on immigration and asylum) at odds with the rest of the European Union.

These diverging attitudes brought the EU to a crossroads: European countries willing to put into practice their commitment to the protection of human rights could do so only by alienating other member states, thus contributing to both the perception and the reality of a democratic deficit. The lack of comprehensive central regulation compounded the problem, given that inconsistencies in relying on either consensus or a qualified majority vote increased the perception that western states were imposing their will on the rest of the EU. As a result, some states refused to endorse decisions even when those decisions would have benefited them. For example, Hungary's Prime Minister Orban claimed that his objection to mandatory quotas was motivated by his belief that such allocations would attract many more asylum seekers and the EU would soon witness "tens of millions" of such individuals at its borders (quoted in "Europe is Finally" 2015). Yet Hungary's decision not to participate in the Council decision of September 22 was to its own detriment since the Commission's original proposal envisioned the relocation of 15,600 individuals from Italy, 50,400 from Greece, and 54,000 from Hungary. With Hungary's refusal to participate, the 54,000 asylum seekers would now be relocated from other countries on the basis of proportional relocation, leaving Hungary in charge of processing the applications of all asylum seekers entering through its territory. In addition to refusing to support the relocation quotas, Hungary and Slovakia also subsequently challenged the Council decision of September 22 before the Court of Justice, claiming that the Council, in making the decision, violated relevant treaties and overstepped its responsibilities (see Hungary v Council 2015; Slovak Republic v Council 2015).[8]

In addition to such political and legal challenges to the relocation scheme, an unwillingness of these member states to participate in the relocation procedures led to inconsistent implementation of the scheme. The agreement envisaged that 66,000 refugees would be relocated in the first year, with the remainder to be relocated in the second year. By May of 2016, however, only 1,500 individuals had been relocated and, by July, the number had only reached 3,056, with Austria, Hungary, Poland, and Slovakia having taken none (European Commission 2016). Orban again reiterated the need for the EU to reconsider its immigration and asylum strategies in order to protect its Christian identity: "Everything which is now taking place before our eyes threatens to have explosive consequences for the whole of Europe . . . We must acknowledge that the European Union's misguided immigration policy is responsible for this situation," he argued (Noack 2015; see also "Orban the Archetype" 2015).

In short, the inability of states to find a solution that would allow the EU to fulfill its obligations under the Geneva Convention and at the same time be acceptable to all member states led to a delayed response and forced countries to resort to improvised unilateral solutions. For instance, Germany on its own decided to allow refugees gathered in Hungary to proceed into its territory and offered to host Syrian refugees regardless of where they first entered the Union. "If Europe fails on the question of refugees, then [Europe's] close link with universal civil rights will be destroyed and it won't be the Europe we wished for," warned the German Chancellor, Angela Merkel, while calling for a united approach and a humanitarian solution (quoted in Feher et al. 2015).

Even this did not work, however. Instead of providing much-needed relief to peripheral states, Germany's decision resulted in a rise in the numbers of asylum seekers arriving at the EU's borders with the goal of reaching Germany. For its part, Hungary welcomed Germany's decision, and took advantage of it by allowing thousands of refugees to proceed, without registering them or processing their asylum applications. In response, the German Chancellor quickly reversed her earlier decision, claiming that Germany's open door policy did not absolve the peripheral states of the responsibility of processing asylum applications (Feher et al. 2015). Soon after, Germany began implementing border controls and document checks, preventing asylum seekers from entering its territory without proper documentation from the country of first entry. While Germany's decision to do so was an extraordinary measure allowed in crisis situations under the Schengen Borders Code (see European Commission 2015f), its action was followed by similar responses elsewhere. Border controls soon emerged in Austria, Slovenia, Sweden, Denmark, and other countries (see European Commission 2015a, 2015g). This marked a temporary end to the principle of freedom of movement that was one of the main foundations of the ambitious European project.

In the end, the major steps in alleviating the pressures of the crisis were not taken within the EU, but between the EU and non-member states affected by the crisis. Recognizing the inability of the EU to manage the crisis on its own, the President of the Commission assembled a meeting of European leaders, of both EU and non-EU states affected by, or party to, the crisis. The outcome of the meeting was an agreement on 17 points of cooperation, including preventing refugees from proceeding to another country's borders without prior consultation with that country and ensuring the biometric registration of all asylum seekers (European Commission 2015b).[9] The goal was to improve communication and cooperation among the countries that were most affected by transit through their territories, as well as to stem the flow of refugees by taking control of entry and secondary transfer of people. After a similar agreement was reached with Turkey (see the Karakatsanis article in this volume), the number of individuals reaching the EU's borders decreased significantly, relieving the pressures on the peripheral states' borders.

Conclusion

The current refugee crisis has created a number of challenges for the European Union. In addition to the difficulties associated with absorbing over 1.3 million individuals in just one year, the crisis was compounded by the fact that existing internal divisions within the EU among member states became apparent, revealing the pitfalls of the EU's growing membership and its expansion to the east. The most striking difference in the responses of EU member states has been between the "original" EU-15 and the relatively recently admitted East European member states. While the former have for the most part responded with empathy for asylum seekers and demonstrated a willingness to fulfill their commitment to protect those endangered in their countries of origin, the new East European members resisted such attempts with calls to protect Europe's Christian identity and culture (see Birnbaum and Witte 2015; Noack 2015; "Orban the Archetype" 2015). Concerned with the effects of the crisis on their cultural values, economic growth, and stability, these countries vowed to defend Europe and its identity by erecting barriers to keep unwanted people out.

In short, although immigration and asylum policies had been transferred to the first pillar of EU decision-making, full institutionalization of these policies was still lacking at the onset of the crisis. This lack of comprehensive regulation and central authority limited EU institutions' ability to respond to the crisis and allowed states to freely design their individual responses, revealing the divergence of interests and values within the EU. While the Commission attempted to take an active approach to resolving the crisis,[10] member states' diverging interests prevented the Council from making significant decisions. Even when decisions were made, they provoked a backlash, court hearings, and even harsher criticisms of the European Union and its response. Thus while the EU-15 began by approaching the refugee crisis cautiously in an attempt to find solutions acceptable to all member states, in the absence of cooperation it ultimately veered toward fulfilling international obligations even at the expense of unity.

Thus, the refugee crisis not only exposed the existence of divisions within the EU, but created a puzzle for its future. An acceleration of integration and greater institutionalization of all policy areas would increase the efficiency of future responses; at the same time, however, efforts to integrate that touch on cultural identity as well as national security are likely to be met with resistance. As a result, both the short-term and long-term integration efforts of the European Union and its enlargement are challenged by such crises and their effects, as member states' inconsistent and varying levels of commitment to the ideals of tolerance and humanitarianism will continue to bring into question the viability of a borderless Europe. While the current crisis is unlikely to signal an end to the European Union, it is likely to bring into question its current membership and institutional structure.

At this time, those committed to protecting refugees and their rights appear to have two options: to respect member states' wishes and violate their own international commitments or to fulfill international obligations, showing empathy for endangered populations but at the same time jeopardize the unity of the European borderless project. Commission President Jean-Claude Juncker suggested that the institutional structure of the EU should be reorganized to account for two groups of states acting at different speeds and with different priorities: "One day we should rethink the European architecture with a group of countries that will do things, all things, together, and others that will position themselves in an orbit away from the core" (European Commission 2015d). What this would appear to signal is a step away from integration. While such a step might not necessarily point to a dissolution of the European Union, allowing for two European "Unions" acting at different speeds and with different interests would significantly alter the borderless structure of the association. A striking divergence of responses, core values, and interests of the member states, exemplified by the refugee crisis, certainly points to that possibility. It is, however, unlikely that such an arrangement would maintain the shared core commitment of the EU to freedom and human rights. What is likely is that such a shift will not be necessary as the EU proceeds with integration at a slow pace. Given that 13 new countries were admitted into the union over the last 12 years, the lack of a coordinated central response was to be expected.

Notes

1. The Maastricht Treaty established a three-pillar structure, dividing policy areas into supranational and intergovernmental categories. The issues within the first, supranational pillar, encompassed policy areas under the control of EU institutions. The second and third pillars, which included Common Foreign and Security Policy and Justice and Home Affairs, were subject to intergovernmental negotiations and decision-making. The three-pillar structure was abolished by the Lisbon Treaty in 2009 as more policy areas were transferred to the supranational decision-making level.
2. The 1990 Convention was replaced in 2003 and again in 2013 with amended Dublin Regulations. See Council of the European Union (2003) "Council Regulation (Ec) No 343/2003 of 18 February 2003 Establishing the Criteria and Mechanisms for Determining the Member State Responsible for Examining an Asylum Application Lodged in One of the Member States by a Third-Country National." *Official Journal of the European Union* L 050.; European Union (2013) "Regulation (Eu) No 604/2013 of the European Parliament and of the Council Establishing the Criteria and Mechanisms for Determining the Member State Responsible for Examining an Application for International Protection Lodged in One of the Member States by a Third-Country National or a Stateless Person (Recast)." Ibid. L 180/31.
3. According to article 73o, for the first five years following the entry into force of the Treaty, all issues in the area of visa, asylum, and immigration policy would require the Council to make decisions unanimously, while after the period of five years, decisions on issues concerning the crossing of external EU borders, border controls, and visa issuance would be made by a qualified majority vote. This was further modified by Article 78(2) TFEU, placing visa, immigration, and asylum policies in their entirety under the jurisdiction of the European Parliament and the Council, which would act in accordance with the ordinary legislative procedure.
4. For a partial list of regulations adopted after the Amsterdam Treaty, see European Commission: Migration and Home Affairs (2016).
5. Under Protocols 21 and 22 TFEU, Denmark, Ireland, and the United Kingdom do not participate in the adoption and application of any measure proposed under Title V, Area of Freedom, Security, and Justice of TFEU.
6. The data are for EU 28, Norway, and Switzerland.
7. Relocation refers to the transfer of asylum seekers within the European Union while resettlement refers to the transfer of individuals from outside the borders of the EU.
8. Specifically, the cases list Article 68 TFEU which designates the European Council as the body responsible for defining "the strategic guidelines for legislative and operational planning within the area of freedom, security, and justice," while Article 13(2) TEU constrains each EU institution to act within the limits of powers designated to it. Additionally, Article 78(3) TFEU authorizes the Council only to adopt provisional measures on a proposal from the Commission, and Article 293(1) TFEU obligates the Council to act under unanimity if Commission proposes such a decision.
9. In addition to leaders of Albania, Austria, Bulgaria, Croatia, FYR Macedonia, Germany, Greece, Hungary, Romania, Serbia, and Slovenia, the meeting was also attended by the President of the European Council, the Luxembourg Presidency of the Council of the EU, the future Dutch Presidency of the Council of the EU, the United Nations High Commissioner for Refugees, and representatives of the European Asylum Support Office and Frontex.
10. For a full list of Commission proposals submitted to the European Parliament and the Council in relation the European Agenda on Migration, see European Commission: Migration and Home Affairs. 2016. "European Agenda on Migration: Legislative Documents." Retrieved January 15, 2017 (http://ec.europa.eu/dgs/home-affairs/what-we-do/policies/european-agenda-migration/proposal-implementation-package/index_en.htm).

References

Birnbaum, Michael and Griff Witte. 2015. "'People in Europe Are Full of Fear' over Refugee Influx." *Washington Post*, September 3. Retrieved March 17, 2017 (www.washingtonpost.com/world/hungarys-leader-to-migrants-please-dont-come/2015/09/03/d5244c6d-53d8-4e82-b9d7-35ec41ca2944_story.html?utm_term=.595783b42b5c).

Council of the European Union. 2001. "Council Directive 2001/55/Ec of 20 July 2001 on Minimum Standards for Giving Temporary Protection in the Event of a Mass Influx of Displaced Persons and on Measures Promoting a Balance of Efforts between Member States in Receiving Such Persons and Bearing the Consequences Thereof." *Official Journal of the European Communities* L 212/12. Retrieved March 17, 2017 (http://eur-lex.europa.eu/legal-content/EN/TXT/?uri=celex:32001L0055).

Council of the European Union. 2003. "Council Regulation (Ec) No 343/2003 of 18 February 2003 Establishing the Criteria and Mechanisms for Determining the Member State Responsible for Examining an Asylum Application Lodged in One of the Member States by a Third-Country National." *Official Journal of the European Union* L 050. Retrieved March 17, 2017 (http://eur-lex.europa.eu/legal-content/EN/TXT/?uri=CELEX:32003R0343).

Council of the European Union. 2004. "Council Directive 2004/83/Ec of 29 April 2004 on Minimum Standards for the Qualification and Status of Third Country Nationals or Stateless Persons as Refugees or as Persons Who Otherwise Need International Protection and the Content of the Protection Granted." *Official Journal of the European Union* L 304/12. Retrieved March 17, 2017 (http://eur-lex.europa.eu/legal-content/EN/TXT/?uri=CELEX%3A32004L0083).

Council of the European Union. 2011. "Council Directive 2003/109/Ec of 25 November 2003 Concerning the Status of Third-Country Nationals Who Are Long-Term Residents as Amended by Directive 2011/51/Eu of the European Parliament and of the Council of 11 May 2011 Amending Council Directive 2003/109/Ec to Extend Its Scope to Beneficiaries of International Protection." *Official Journal of the European Union* L 132/1. Retrieved November 16, 2016 (http://eur-lex.europa.eu/legal-content/EN/TXT/?uri=CELEX:32011L0051).

Council of the European Union. 2015a. "Council Decision (Eu) 2015/1523 of 14 September 2015 Establishing Provisional Measures in the Area of International Protection for the Benefit of Italy and of Greece." *Official Journal of the European Union* L 239:146–56. Retrieved January 21, 2017 (http://eur-lex.europa.eu/legal-content/EN/TXT/?uri=OJ%3AJOL_2015_239_R_0011).

Council of the European Union. 2015b. "Council Decision (Eu) 2015/1601 of 22 September 2015 Establishing Provisional Measures in the Area of International Protection for the Benefit of Italy and Greece." *Official Journal of the European Union* L 248:80–94. Retrieved March 23, 2017 (http://eur-lex.europa.eu/legal-content/EN/TXT/?uri=celex%3A32015D1601).

"Europe is Finally Confronting the Migrant Crisis: Hungary's Outspoken Prime Minister Has Spurred Europe into Action." 2015. *The Economist*, September 4. Retrieved January 12, 2017 (www.economist.com/news/europe/21663496-hungarys-outspoken-prime-minister-has-spurred-europe-action-europe-finally-confronting).

European Asylum Support Office. 2015. "Quarterly Asylum Report: Quarter 1, 2015." Retrieved November 4, 2016 (www.easo.europa.eu/information-analysis/analysis-and-statistics/quarterly-asylum-report/).

European Asylum Support Office. 2016. "Information & Analysis: Latest Asylum Trends." Retrieved November 4, 2016 (www.easo.europa.eu/latest-asylum-trends).

European Commission. 2015a. "European Commission Statement Following the Temporary Reintroduction of Controls by Slovenia at the Border with Hungary." Brussels. Retrieved March 17, 2017 (http://europa.eu/rapid/press-release_STATEMENT-15-5667_en.htm).
European Commission. 2015b. "Meeting on the Western Balkans Migration Route: Leaders Agree on 17-Point Plan of Action." Brussels. Retrieved March 17, 2017 (http://europa.eu/rapid/press-release_IP-15-5904_en.htm).
European Commission. 2015c. "A European Agenda on Migration: Communication from the Commission to the European Parliament, the Council, the European Economic and Social Committee and the Committee of the Regions, Com(2015) 240." Brussels. May 13. Retrieved February 23, 2017 (http://ec.europa.eu/dgs/home-affairs/what-we-do/policies/european-agenda-migration/index_en.htm).
European Commission. 2015d. "Citizens' Dialogue 2015 in Brussels, with the Participation of Jean-Claude Juncker." Retrieved February 20, 2017 (http://ec.europa.eu/avservices/video/player.cfm?ref=I111775&sitelang=EN).
European Commission. 2015e. "Proposal for a Council Decision Establishing Provisional Measures in the Area of International Protection for the Benefit of Italy, Greece and Hungary." *COM(2015) 451*, September 9. Retrieved February 12, 2017 (http://eur-lex.europa.eu/legal-content/EN/TXT/?uri=CELEX%3A52015PC0451).
European Commission. 2015f. "European Commission Statement Following the Temporary Reintroduction of Border Controls by Germany, Particularly at the German-Austrian Border." Retrieved September 13, 2016 (http://europa.eu/rapid/press-release_STATEMENT-15-5638_en.htm).
European Commission. 2015g. "European Commission Statement Following the Temporary Reintroduction of Border Controls by Austria, Particularly at the Hungarian-Austrian Border." Brussels. Retrieved February 17, 2017 (http://europa.eu/rapid/press-release_STATEMENT-15-5648_en.htm).
European Commission. 2016. "Relocation and Resettlement: State of Play." Brussels, May 13. Retrieved February 21, 2017 (https://ec.europa.eu/home-affairs/what-we-do/policies/european-agenda-migration/background-information_en).
European Commission: Migration and Home Affairs. 2016. "European Agenda on Migration: Legislative Documents." Retrieved January 15, 2017 (http://ec.europa.eu/dgs/home-affairs/what-we-do/policies/european-agenda-migration/proposal-implementation-package/index_en.htm).
European Council. 1999. "Tampere European Council 15–16 October 1999 Presidency Conclusions." Retrieved November 17, 2016 (www.europarl.europa.eu/summits/tam_en.htm).
European Council. 2015. "Special Meeting of the European Council, 23 April." Retrieved February 1, 2017 (www.consilium.europa.eu/en/press/press-releases/2015/04/23-special-euco-statement/).
European Parliament. 2015. "Resolution on the Latest Tragedies in the Mediterranean and Eu Migration and Asylum Policies." *2015/2660(RSP)*. Retrieved January 11, 2017 (www.europarl.europa.eu/oeil/popups/ficheprocedure.do?lang=en&reference=2015/2660(RSP)).
European Union. 1990. "Convention Determining the State Responsible for Examining Applications for Asylum Lodged in One of the Member States of the European Communities: Dublin Convention." *Official Journal of the European Union* C 254. June 15, 1990, entered into force August 19 1997. Retrieved October 16, 2016 (http://eur-lex.europa.eu/legal-content/EN/ALL/?uri=celex%3A41997A0819(01)).
European Union. 1997. "Treaty of Amsterdam Amending the Treaty on European Union, the Treaties Establishing the European Communities and Certain Related Acts." *Official*

Journal of the European Communities C 340(1):1–144. Retrieved March 23, 2017 (http://eur-lex.europa.eu/legal-content/EN/TXT/?uri=CELEX%3A11997D%2FAFI).

European Union. 2011. "Directive 2011/95/Eu of the European Parliament and of the Council of 13 December 2011 on Standards for the Qualification of Third-Country Nationals or Stateless Persons as Beneficiaries of International Protection, for a Uniform Status for Refugees or for Persons Eligible for Subsidiary Protection, and for the Content of the Protection Granted (Recast)." *Official Journal of the European Union* L 337/9. Retrieved March 17, 2017 (http://eur-lex.europa.eu/legal-content/en/TXT/?uri=celex%3A32011L0095).

European Union. 2012. "Consolidated Version of the Treaty on the Functioning of the European Union." *Official Journal of the European Union* C 326:1–390. Retrieved March 17, 2017 (http://eur-lex.europa.eu/legal-content/en/TXT/?uri=CELEX:12012E/TXT).

European Union. 2013. "Regulation (Eu) No 604/2013 of the European Parliament and of the Council Establishing the Criteria and Mechanisms for Determining the Member State Responsible for Examining an Application for International Protection Lodged in One of the Member States by a Third-Country National or a Stateless Person (Recast)." *Official Journal of the European Union* L 180/31. Retrieved March 17, 2017 (http://eur-lex.europa.eu/legal-content/en/ALL/?uri=celex%3A32013R0604).

Eurostat. 2016. "Asylum Statistics." Retrieved September 2, 2016 (http://ec.europa.eu/eurostat/statistics-explained/index.php/Asylum_statistics).

Feher, Margit, Andrea Thomas, and Ruth Bender. 2015. "Europe's Migrant Crackdown: Chaos Reigns as Austria, Hungary Move to Slow Flow: Merkel Warns of Need to Share Burden." *Wall Street Journal.* Retrieved September 12, 2016 (http://search.proquest.com.libaccess.sjlibrary.org/docview/1708458139?accountid=10361).

Hungary v. Council of the European Union. 2015. *Case C-647/15: Court of Justice of the European Union.* Retrieved March 17, 2017 (http://eur-lex.europa.eu/legal-content/EN/TXT/?uri=CELEX%3A62015CN0647).

Noack, Rick. 2015. "Muslims Threaten Europe's Christian Identity, Hungary's Leader Says." *The Washington Post World Views,* September 3. Retrieved February 2, 2017 (www.washingtonpost.com/news/worldviews/wp/2015/09/03/muslims-threaten-europes-christian-identity-hungarys-leader-says/).

"Orban the Archetype: Eastern European Attitudes." 2015. *The Economist* 416:48–9.

Popescu, Alexandra. 2016. "The E.U. 'Costs' of the Refugee Crisis." *Europolity* 10(1):105–20.

Presidency of the Council of the European Union. 2015. "Extraordinary Jha Council: The Ministers Adopted by a Qualified Majority the Provisional Mechanism for the Emergency Relocation of 120,000 Persons in Need of International Protection." Retrieved January 12, 2017 (www.eu2015lu.eu/en/actualites/articles-actualite/2015/09/22-conseil-jai-extra/).

Roberts, Bayard, Adrianna Murphy, and Martin McKee. 2016. "Europe's Collective Failure to Address the Refugee Crisis." *Public Health Reviews (2107–6952)* 37:1–5.

Selanec, Nika Bačić. 2015. "A Critique of E.U. Refugee Crisis Management: On Law, Policy and Decentralisation." *Croatian Yearbook of European Law & Policy* 11:73–114.

Slovak Republic v. Council of the European Union. 2015. *Case C-643/15: Court of Justice of the European Union.* Retrieved March 17, 2017 (http://eur-lex.europa.eu/legal-content/EN/TXT/?uri=CELEX%3A62015CN0643).

Troianovski, Anton, Emmerentze Jervell Ellen, and Margit Feher. 2015. "Europe Borders Tighten in Chain Reaction: Countries Follow German Move on Reinstating ID Checks, Triggering Rush to Cross." *Wall Street Journal: Eastern Edition* 266:A11.

United Nations. 1951. "Convention Relating to the Status of Refugees." *United Nations Treaty Series* 189:137.

United Nations. 1967. "Protocol Relating to the Status of Refugees." *United Nations Treaty Series* 606:267.

8

FROM TECHNOLOGIES OF CONTROL TO "FACEBOOK REFUGEES"

The Unintended Consequences of the EU-Turkey Agreement on the Refugee Crisis in Greece[1]

Neovi M. Karakatsanis

INDIANA UNIVERSITY SOUTH BEND

> *Political and Military Sociology: An Annual Review*, 2017, Vol. 45: 122–141.
>
> *This article takes a critical look at the policy challenges facing the EU and Greece, the Mediterranean country that has served as a major recipient of refugees crossing into Europe from Turkey. Based on preliminary observations on one of the receiving islands, the article analyzes some of the unintended consequences of the EU-Turkey Agreement, including the increased costs and physical dangers of refugees who attempt the crossing, the worsening of conditions in Greek refugee camps, the violent clashes between Syrians, Afghans, and other refugees in Greece, increased xenophobia among the Greek population, as well as the increased use of technology by migrants to evade border control and to facilitate migration. The article concludes that, as the "gap hypothesis" has illustrated in other settings, a notable divergence exists between the stated intentions of EU policy and its actual results.*

Since January 2015, Greece, one of the main entry points for refugees and migrants in Europe, has seen over one million people—the vast majority from Syria, Iraq, and Afghanistan—cross its borders clandestinely on their way to northern Europe (see Lamb 2016). Risking their lives at sea, the vast majority of these refugees arrived on Lesbos, an island about 4 miles from the Turkish coast, with the rest entering via one of the other Aegean islands also close to Turkey. Viewing Greece as a transit country to one of the more prosperous northern European states, most refugees and migrants remained temporarily in Greece, thanks in large part to Greek policy that allowed asylum seekers to circumvent the Dublin Regulation.[2]

This situation changed dramatically in March and April 2016 when, as discussed elsewhere in this volume, a number of European countries and the European Union itself increased border policing. Specifically, a series of border closures in countries to the north of Greece and, subsequently, an agreement between the European Union and Turkey trapped over 60,000 undocumented migrants and asylum seekers in the country. I argue that the outcomes of the EU-Turkish Agreement signal a gap between the intended and unintended consequences of the EU's efforts to stem migratory flows. Based on material from a variety of sources, including published scholarly research, reports produced by a number of NGOs/IGOs, an analysis of media reports, and personal observations on one of the receiving islands, I maintain that the EU's policy resulted in a number of unintended consequences, negatively affecting individuals arriving on the shores of Greece, as well as the native Greek islanders who initially welcomed them. Intended to stem the flow of migration, the EU-Turkey Agreement pushed migrants and refugees into the hands of even more ruthless human smugglers who were willing to take greater risks with human life, entrapped migrants in Greek refugee camps that were ill-prepared to provide for their daily needs, contributed to increased animosity and unrest among various ethnic groups residing in the camps, and turned many once-compassionate Greek islanders into hostile adversaries of migration.

Virginie Guiraudon and Christian Joppke have argued that policy gaps (such as those experienced in Greece) often result when immigration policies attempt to stem migration flows (see Guiraudon and Joppke 2001; Joppke 2004; Cornelius and Tsuda 2004). Such gaps can be brought about by the unintended consequences of policy as well as the inadequate enforcement or implementation of policy. One cause of this, according to Wayne Cornelius and Takeyuki Tsuda, is that

> states themselves are fragmentary and do not speak in a uniform voice. This is especially true when immigration policy making involves a large number of governmental agencies with different (if not conflicting) agendas and constituencies. . . . Additional problems result from the fact that the government agencies that make policy are frequently different from those who implement it (2004: 14).

The case of policy-making and policy implementation in Greece and the EU is a prime example of this phenomenon, made all the more pronounced by the fact that policy-making is taking place at the supranational level, while implementation occurs at the hands of national governments in remote borderlands (see Cabot 2014). In such a context, it is hardly surprising that the unintended consequences described below have come to exist.

A second contributing factor to the policy gap between immigration control policies and outcomes has resulted from the fact that elected political officials—in the European Union and in its member states—act on a public mandate to restrict border crossings. To do so, they must convey the impression to a wary electorate that Europe's common southern border is sufficiently protected from illegal flows of migration (see Andreas 2009). However, to fully realize the public's mandate, European elites would have to abandon some of the very principles and international conventions—for example, the European Convention on Human Rights and the Geneva Convention on the Status of Refugees—that European states and, indeed, the EU as an institution have shaped and promoted. As Heath Cabot argues,

> [G]iven Greece's status as a European external border, asylum in Greece . . . threw into crisis the EU capacity both to protect European territories and citizens from "alien" threats and to comply with international laws guaranteeing protection for persons fleeing violence and persecution (2014: 4).

Not able or willing to abandon the democratic values enshrined in liberal international conventions, European policy-makers are caught in a bind, attempting to convey the image of an EU that continues to uphold human rights, while at the same time projecting another image of control. Caught between these two competing goals and, as I argue, in the face of technological advances that have contributed to the democratization of migration and the evasion of borders, European policy has resulted in inadvertent consequences.

In short, as a result of the fragmentary and dichotomous nature of the European Union—policy being made at the supranational level but implemented at the national level, as well as its commitment to liberal democratic principles in the face of the public mandate to restrict refugee and migrant flows—serious policy gaps have led to the unintended consequences discussed in this article. After a brief introduction to the background of the closing of borders that has entrapped over 60,000 refugees and other migrants in Greece, I turn to a discussion of some of the unintended consequences caused by the immigration policy gap.

The Background: The Closing of the Balkan and Aegean Routes

In the face of massive refugee movements of a scale not seen since the end of World War II, a number of European countries, particularly in the Balkans, took measures in early 2016 to reinstate border controls by erecting barbed wire border fences, mobilizing their militaries to guard external borders, and augmenting their manpower contributions to Frontex, the EU's external borders agency. By February of that year, such measures had brought about the closure of the so-called "Balkan Route," the route that had been taken by undocumented migrants and refugees who entered the European Union via Greece and slowly moved north through the Balkans until they reached their final destination in one of Europe's northern, more prosperous states. This closure caused an immense bottleneck on Greece's border with the Former Yugoslav Republic of Macedonia, where tens of thousands of migrants converged, waiting for a border reopening.

In March 2016, the bottleneck worsened when the European Union and Turkey proceeded to sign an accord, further escalating control measures. Designed to deter clandestine sea crossings across the Mediterranean and to foil the work of human traffickers, the agreement all but closed the "Aegean Route," the path that was being taken by refugees and other migrants in small inflatable boats from Turkey to the Greek islands in the Aegean Sea. According to the EU-Turkey Agreement, all undocumented migrants who henceforth arrived on one of these islands would no longer be allowed to travel by ferry to the mainland and from there to a North European destination. Instead, they would now have to apply for asylum on the islands and, if unsuccessful in their bid, would be returned to Turkey.

To return undocumented migrants and unsuccessful asylum claimants to Turkey and to de-incentivize future clandestine crossings, a "fast-track" process for handling asylum claims was to be set up in Greece and refugee reception centers were to be converted to closed detention camps. Refugees and other migrants would not be allowed to leave the camps during the asylum process. Instead, they would be individually interviewed in the camps by an asylum officer (typically supplied by Frontex), and Greek judges would rule on all appeals. Only those individuals able to prove they were at risk if returned to either their country of origin or to Turkey would be permitted to remain in Europe.[3] With Turkish cooperation, the agreement was a European Union attempt to address significant popular resistance to the large influx of Muslim immigrants to Europe. To what extent did this European Union policy accomplish its intended outcomes? It is to this question that I now turn.

The EU-Turkey Agreement: Success or Failure?

Without question, it would appear that at least over the short-term, the EU-Turkey deal did provide the European Union with increased control over its common borders in the Aegean Sea. Indeed, the agreement drastically reduced the number of refugees entering the EU via Greece through the Aegean. Existing data illustrate this quite well. While 42,601 and 31,416 refugees arrived on the Aegean island of Lesbos in January and February 2016, respectively, only 14,155 and 1,766 arrived there in March and April 2016 (Pazianou 2016). Data provided by the International Organization for Migration also confirm this downward trend, substantiating that average daily landings in Greece from Turkey fell drastically from 2,056 in January 2016 to just 47 in May of that year (DW 2016). Thus, in important respects, the EU's objective of closing the Aegean border to new arrivals by sea was successful. However, success was not achieved without consequence.

The Strengthening of Smuggling Networks

It is a well-known fact that, as a result of tougher policies making it increasingly difficult to enter the European Union legally as an economic migrant or asylum seeker, the practice of many migrants has been to seek illicit routes. This has been no different for those arriving through the Aegean Route to Greece. By closing off legal forms of migration and asylum, European policy-makers have unwittingly contributed to the solidification of a billion-dollar smuggling industry and, thereby, a loss of border control. This agreement has thus pushed smuggling operations elsewhere in the Mediterranean, likely strengthening the largest, most powerful, and most ruthless smuggling networks. To illustrate the plight of refugees who find themselves in the hands of such smugglers, I turn to the circumstances faced by refugees and other migrants making the Aegean crossing.

First, many refugees and other migrants pay human smugglers[4] multiple times as they transit from their country of origin to their country of destination. Depending on the refugee's finances, some arrange for smugglers to supply them with a passport and airline ticket to their destination (about $3,880 per person), while others make the crossing from Greece into FYROM by land for less than half that cost (about $1,500). Based on refugee accounts, the more secure a refugee is financially, the fewer the number of smugglers he or she will rely on in transit; a counterfeit passport and airline ticket to a desired north European destination from the Middle East may suffice for the financially secure. However, the less affluent will have a longer trip—one with multiple smugglers along the way. For example, an Afghan refugee who worked as a contractor for UK and U.S. forces in Afghanistan and who later fled with his wife and four children is typical. Having paid smugglers $750 per person to guide his family over the mountains from Iran into Turkey, he gave a second smuggler $1,000 per person to take the family from Istanbul to Izmir. From there, he and his family were taken by yet another smuggler to the Greek island of Chios by boat for an additional fee (Margaronis 2016).

Once in Greece, most migrants continue to pay for the services of several more smugglers along the way before they reach their final European destination. On Greece's northern border, smugglers—oftentimes Moroccan, Algerian, or Afghan—trawl refugee camps at night, selling their "services" for about another $1,660 (Squires 2016). An 18-year-old Syrian boy confirms, "I'm looking for a smuggler. . . . Everyone here is trying to get a smuggler and move from [here], by plane or by walking, or anything else" (quoted in Japan Times

2016). This pattern of hiring not one but a series of smugglers has become commonplace. In addition, migrants often have to make several attempts to cross the same border before they succeed. In such instances, migrants are forced to pay smugglers multiple times for the same crossing:

> We sold everything we had in Afghanistan including our home. . . . [W]hen the Macedonian police caught my younger brother and me crossing the border with Serbia (sic). Just a day after they sent us back to Greece, we were heading north again. Soon we were on our way again and smugglers transported us to Horgos where we reunited with our family. . . . We have to move further to the EU now as quickly as we can. Even if the Hungarian police send us back, we will try to go through Romania. We won't give up until we have reached Switzerland (Mahmud, quoted in Tomic 2016).

In short, given the high cost of smuggling, the multiple borders that must be crossed clandestinely, and the fact that initial crossings are often foiled, it is not uncommon for such determined migrants to pay tens of thousands of dollars for smuggling services.

While the costs of being smuggled are exorbitant, the power that smugglers wield over the lives of refugees is even greater. In addition to putting their lives at risk as they are forced to make sea crossings in inclement weather in overcrowded inflatable boats, many refugees are also gravely mistreated on the journey. One refugee describes the following all-too-common situation:

> [O]n the ship, the smugglers took our mobile phones, and locked us in for most of the journey . . . they didn't give us food or water for 36 hours. Moreover, there was no toilet on our deck. . . . The ship was decent, but the weather was severe. At one point, a nine-meter high wave broke the window of our ship and water came in. Everyone was crying, vomiting, and some lost consciousness a few times. We were all scared and thought we were going to die (quoted in IOM 2016).

In another account, a Syrian doctor faced a beating with a metal cane when he demanded that his money be returned to him after a foiled crossing. Another refugee describes what the doctor experienced as well as his own interaction with the same smuggler,

> I saw [the doctor] after the beating. . . . [H]is eye was badly swollen. . . . [The smuggler told me,] if you leave, you're going to lose fifteen hundred dollars, as a penalty. . . . I couldn't afford that, and he also hinted that I'd be beaten up, just like the doctor was. I was losing all hope. My money was gone, and I was tied down with [this smuggler] (quoted in Schmidle 2015).

Human smuggling is replete with such abuse: fake lifejackets, unseaworthy boats, extortion, abandonment at sea, and even "pirates"—men who board the boats, steal the motors, and rob refugees of all their possessions. Still worse are the physical and sexual assaults that the most vulnerable individuals—unaccompanied women and children—face.

When interviewed by Amnesty International (2016), unaccompanied women reported having faced financial exploitation, physical abuse, sexual harassment, and pressure to have sex at the hands of smugglers.[5] Some women (particularly those who lack the finances to pay smugglers for their services) speak of being harassed and propositioned by smugglers and their associates who often offer a discounted or shorter trip in return for sex. As one young woman from Aleppo recounted:

> At the hotel in Turkey, one of the men working with the smuggler, a Syrian man, said if I sleep with him, I will not pay or pay less. Of course I said no, it was disgusting. The same happened in Jordan to all of us.

And,

> My friend who came with me from Syria ran out of money in Turkey, so the smuggler's assistant offered her to have sex with him [in exchange for a place on the boat]; she of course said no, and couldn't leave Turkey, so she's staying there (quoted in Amnesty International 2016).

While the stated purpose of the EU-Turkey Agreement was to arrest the work of such smugglers, observers have noted that one consequence of the agreement was that it forced a reopening of other, more expensive, smuggling routes over the Mediterranean Sea into Italy. According to one report, for example, trafficking networks are charging over $5,500 for clandestine sea crossings in larger fishing and cargo vessels into Italy from southern Turkey, increasing daily arrivals from 176 in January 2016 to 643 in May (Chan 2016; DW 2016). As Lucy Carrigan of the International Rescue Committee emphasized: "Pushing people back to Turkey is not the answer—desperate people will find other routes" (quoted in Squires 2016).

Still worse, others emphasize that the central Mediterranean crossing is a far more dangerous and deathly route for migrants. According to the International Organization for Migration, while one of 893 people crossing the Aegean Sea since January 2014 had drowned, the numbers were much higher for those crossing into Italy, with one out of every 54 people losing their life. In addition, smugglers from Libya, from where the most dangerous crossings take place, are notorious for locking people in holds where they are known to suffocate or become trapped in the event of a sinking.

In short, in the attempt to close its borders and convey an image of control, European Union policy has fostered an unintended, potentially deadly consequence, pushing refugees into the hands of even more ruthless trafficking networks and into far more dangerous and life-threatening crossings than those of the Aegean. Unfortunately, this has not been the only unintended consequence.

Conditions in the Camps

In addition to the aforementioned outcome, the agreement, which also required refugees to remain in closed camps in Greece while asylum claims are being processed, brought about a second unintended consequence. As discussed later, the camps in which refugees are required to remain are ill-prepared to meet their needs. Also, because the agreement has forced a spike in asylum requests in Greece, overcrowding is today a serious problem. Lacking the resources and human-power to process a large number of requests in a timely manner, the problem faced by camp officials has been compounded by the lack of European progress in relocating refugees to other European states. Take, for example, the island of Chios, where a single asylum official was assigned to review 500–800 claims. A mounting backlog of claims has led to increased frustration, including hunger strikes and unrest among refugees.

As indicated, the refugee centers have become gravely overcrowded, dilapidated, and unsanitary. As one local official on Chios argued, when the camp hosted refugees for a few days while their claims were being processed for onward movement, the "process was fast, [and] . . . difficulties in the centre were only minor problems. But now, we have people there for many days, and we need to provide different services" (Dimitris Karalis, quoted in Trafford 2016). Unable to provide the "different services" due to a lack of resources, camp conditions reinforce the image of an unwelcoming Europe, one that detains refugees in substandard camps as they await processing.

Fleeing war, violence, and deep poverty in search of a better life in northern Europe, many refugees find themselves in a variety of centers and camps—in European funded "hot spots," formal reception centers, informal refugee camps, and closed detention centers. Many of the camps are little more than tent cities in muddy or dusty fields, while others have been formally but hastily organized by the Greek government in closed warehouses, factories, and army barracks, inside of which tents have been pitched. While camps vary in terms of their location, size, and degree of openness or closure, they all tend to be overcrowded and characterized by poor living conditions. Reports by the United Nations High Commissioner for Refugees (UNHCR) and many non-governmental organizations active in the camps underline the insufficient number of toilets, showers, medical personnel, and translators. Others also allege that some of the camps lack electricity, good air circulation, as well as ample food and water supplies. Still others indicate a lack of provisions for infants, lactating mothers, the elderly, and the disabled. As one British activist put it:

> I've visited a lot of the new camps. . . . Some of them are OK, but some of them are horrific: they're disused factories, they're very dirty, there's flooding, and people are getting one portion of food every day, not three portions (Kingsley 2016).

Another volunteer agreed, "There was no running water or showers or electricity or firewood. Mothers had no hot water for baby formula or to sanitize bottles, and had to use cold water" (Townsend 2016). A third activist noted that, without the provision of WiFi, refugees cannot apply for asylum, which must be done online (Townsend 2016).

Reinforcing such deficiencies is the fact that many mainstream NGOs, as well as the UNHCR, object to closed detention centers and will not work in them, leaving the provision of food and other necessities to the Greek government and its military caterers who are hard pressed to meet the needs of the camps. A member of the Norwegian Refugee Council (NRC) recently justified pulling out of one of Chios's closed detention centers by explaining, "We don't want to support authorities to manage a jail" (Sébastien Daridan of the NRC, quoted in Lopez 2016).

Given the unwillingness of mainstream IGOs and NGOs to work in closed camps, many such centers are managed by the Greek army with assistance from Frontex. As a result, IGOs and NGOs have been displaced by official workers, many of whom lack the know-how and resources to effectively manage the unprecedented humanitarian crisis. Lacking legal experts, translators, and necessary resources, including European humanitarian aid, Greek and European authorities[6] have attempted to handle the crisis with scarce resources. Giorgos Kyritsis, a Greek government spokesperson for Greece's coordinating body of the refugee crisis, has agreed that his government's attempt to deal with the situation has fallen short:

> Every time a new site is opened there are shortages in the beginning but then we add amenities and in due process we resolve them. We're not saying conditions are perfect, we want to improve them but there is absolutely no comparison between the new facilities and Idomeni (the largest informal camp on the Greek border with FYROM that was closed by the government). At least now they have a roof over their head. When it rains they don't get wet and they're not being forced to live in the mud. Surely that's an improvement (quoted in Townsend 2016).

And,

> After the E.U. Turkey agreement, we had to convert these open camps into closed facilities. . . . We had to do it in just two days with limited resources and funding. We want to guarantee the rights of everyone who made it under the E.U.-Turkey status, but we did have some problems (quoted in Lopez 2016).

FIGURES 8.1 and 8.2   A view of the Vial Refugee Camp in Chios, Greece.

FIGURES 8.1 and 8.2 (Continued)

Given the deteriorating living conditions, the long lines for food and other necessities,[7] the continued paucity of information and the uncertainty surrounding the asylum process itself, it is not at all surprising that tensions have increased with periodic eruptions of unrest and violence. As one detainee who arrived in Greece after the EU-Turkey agreement went into effect describes:

> We apply for asylum in Greece. . . . But they don't tell us when the interview will be. One month? Two months? A year? Nobody knows. . . . [The camp] is a jail. . . . Food is terrible. There isn't enough water, we can't wash our clothes. When we are sick, we have to wait three hours to see a doctor. There is fighting every night here. There are too many people (Afghan refugee, quoted in Lopez 2016).

This situation is particularly dire for unaccompanied female migrants who face sexual abuse and other assaults as they attempt to reach a European safe haven.[8] Based on interviews with 40 refugee women and girls who made it to northern Europe, Amnesty International (2016) reported the extent of female insecurity. According to the report, "Women and girls travelling alone and those accompanied only by their children felt particularly under threat in transit areas and camps in Hungary, Croatia, and Greece, where they were forced to sleep alongside hundreds of refugee men, sometimes in the same tent or container." The insecurity was so pervasive that some women preferred to leave the designated areas to sleep instead out in the open. As one woman explained, "Men get drunk and there is no safety. . . . We are also scared that something may happen to our children" (quoted in Kosmopoulos 2016). According to another woman, "The other night a man simply opened the door and tried to come into our room" (quoted in Kosmopoulos 2016). A 19-year-old single Eritrean woman describes a common occurrence:

> The men get drunk and try to enter our tent every night. . . . We went to the police and asked to be taken to a separate part of the camp from the men who try to abuse us, but the police refused to help us. We fled our country for exactly this reason, and here in this camp we are afraid to leave our tent (quoted in Human Rights Watch 2016).

A single Afghan woman has faced a similar experience:

> Yesterday there was a fight between Sunni and Shia Afghans. One Afghan came and threatened me and said, "I will come back at night and rape you." I feel insecure here. They [the police] haven't taken any measures to protect us (quoted in Human Rights Watch 2016).

Because single women are not separated from unrelated adult male refugees in the camps, a common location for voyeurism, sexual harassment, and attempted rape is the showers and bathrooms that are often mixed, unprotected, and that lack proper lighting at night. As one female refugee reported, "I'm so scared, I never leave my room at night" (quoted in Kosmopoulos 2016). Indeed, to avoid relieving themselves after dark, many women report not eating or drinking after a certain hour. Others indicate that they do not go to the bathroom alone and never at night (Amnesty International 2016): "We stay in groups and only go to sleep when we are really tired. In the night, we don't leave our tents and our children are forced to go to the toilet inside" (quoted in Kosmopoulos 2016).

The degrading situations many migrants face has given rise to unrest in the camps. Riots regularly erupt, tents are set on fire, and many refugees break out of the centers, preferring to live in informal makeshift camps.[9] However, as I illustrate below, the departure of refugees from the camps has not been without incident. On the island of Chios, reports of refugees trampling crops and stealing chickens, eggs, beans, and other foodstuffs quickly spread among the local population. In addition, fights—typically between young Syrian and Afghan men armed with rocks, bottles, and razor blades—break out. In one such incident in April 2016, 600 people escaped from a closed camp and six individuals were hospitalized as a result of the clashes.[10] As frustrations grew, buildings in the camp were ransacked, windows smashed, tents set on fire, and equipment broken. In many ways, then, the EU-Turkey Agreement that was intended to give the impression of border control and authority has instead led to mounting frustration, unrest, and even violence among refugees, giving Greek observers the impression of a loss of control and authority in Greece—another unintended consequence of the Agreement.

The Repercussions of Migrant Unrest on Native Attitudes

Another indicator of a policy gap is increasingly negative public opinion towards migrants and refugees. As Cornelius and Tsuda write, "[T]he wider the policy gap, the stronger the public backlash. . . . [T]he public may feel that the government has lost control of immigration and react negatively" (2004: 6). Indeed, in Greece migrant unrest has fueled anti-migrant attitudes among indigenous Greeks—many of whom had previously evinced empathy and compassion towards the refugees, helping with sea rescues and donating necessities, such as food, blankets, and clothing, often taking clothes off of their own children to hand over to wet and tired newcomers (Lamb 2016: 73). In fact, so extensive were the humanitarian efforts of ordinary people on the Greek islands that solidarity movements representing thousands of anonymous islanders were collectively nominated for the 2016 Nobel Peace Prize. According to the nomination letter, which garnered well over a half million signatures,

> [W]hen faced with the actual pain of refugees on the ground, the residents of the islands on the frontline have responded, in their majority, with overwhelming empathy and self-sacrifice. They fundraised; opened their homes; dove into treacherous waters to save lives; took care of the sick and the injured; shared a meal or their garments with new arrivals. In their effort they were joined by many others: tourists, visitors, activists, and some organized professionals, who came from abroad to help. Hence, it would not be an exaggeration to say that, to a large extent, the worst humanitarian crisis since World War II has been dealt with so far through the unprecedented, spontaneous mobilizations of ordinary, largely-anonymous people. . . . With their tireless action, courage, and empathy, the anonymous volunteers represented by the numerous solidarity networks that

have emerged in the Greek islands exemplify the most precious—and most fragile—ideals of our humanity. . . . Their choice to embrace the "stranger," the "other," the "asylum-seeker" reveals . . . our shared human need for freedom, empathy, and peace (Various Authors 2016).

As one refugee remembered, "They [Greeks] were going through their own [economic] crisis, and they were still kind to us" (quoted in Schmidle 2015). This same refugee recounts the sense of safety he felt his first night in Greece, where he slept on the tiled floor of a natatorium that had been converted into a makeshift reception center:

> That was the best feeling in the world. . . . For the first time in years, I knew that I could sleep without waking up with sweats, from fear. No bombs could fall on my head, no one would try to take me. . . . In Europe, it's better to sleep for two hours than it is to sleep for fifty hours in Syria. Because, in Syria, in each one of those hours you'll have hundreds of nightmares (quoted in Schmidle 2015).

The islanders' "humanity," however, was not to last for long. The EU-Turkey Agreement that closed the Aegean Route, trapping refugees in Greece and turning their frustrations into violent unrest, also turned islanders' compassion to aggravation. As a result, an increasing number of Greek islanders and others have adopted anti-refugee, xenophobic attitudes. The words of one local on the island of Chios reveal the frustration of many whose hospitality turned to resentment:

> In the beginning, when there were maybe 40 of them in the boats, all wet, we helped them. Now they're too many. They steal chickens, they shit in the fields. They threw stones at a woman. . . . Eventually they'll set off a bomb and sink the island (quoted in Margaronis 2016).

Other islanders agree: "In the beginning, we felt sorry for them but, once they started doing what they did, we began not to want them anymore."[11] A third corroborates, "I refuse to give them anything anymore. They're always complaining about the food they are given, and they are very dirty, throwing trash everywhere."[12]

Soon, Greek frustration began to manifest itself in anti-migrant protests. In Chios, for example, locals (joined by members of the neo-fascist Golden Dawn group) violently confronted refugees who had escaped the Vial camp and set up an informal camp at Chios's harbor, and tried to forcibly remove them. Others stormed city hall demanding that the refugees be moved, while still others resorted to throwing Molotov cocktails at a house where volunteers and refugees reside on the island (Webb 2016). As the mayor argued, when the migrants occupied the island's port, "local society felt suffocated" (quoted in Margaronis 2016). Such incidents continue, with camps on several islands being burned to the ground and with ensuing clashes between refugees and the police.

Given the volatility brought on by the entrapment of refugees in Greece, it is not surprising that tensions between refugees and Greek citizens escalated. Add to this the refugee-on-refugee violence and the unrest within the camps themselves, and islanders perceive the refugees as disruptive, undesirable, and uncontrollable guests in their midst. In short, as clashes occur, Greek attitudes toward them worsen. To project an image of control on Europe's southern border, European policy-makers failed to foresee that entrapment of refugees in Greece would lead many of them to believe that their government had lost control of the border, another unintended consequence of the Agreement.

By Way of Conclusion: Democratizing Migration Through the Use of Technologies

To this point, I have argued that the EU-Turkey Agreement, while stemming the flow of migrants and refugees, has left many refugees victims of a policy gap that is the result of a faulty asylum process, one that has led to a number of unintended consequences. Rather than providing refugees with accessible means of claiming asylum at reception centers in Turkey, for example, European policy-makers have focused instead on controlling and closing the Greek-Turkish border. To convey the image of a border under control, policy-makers resorted to greater policing, increased coast guard patrols, and an agreement with Turkey intended to reduce the number of refugees and migrants smuggled across the Aegean. This article has argued that a number of adverse unintended consequences ensued: the use of even more ruthless smugglers and dangerous routes, the entrapment of refugees in camps that have grown increasingly unsanitary and overcrowded, increased animosities within the camps between various ethnic and religious groups, the victimization of women, and growing xenophobia among the native population. Clearly, the EU-Turkey Agreement is in these respects a failed policy.

In this section, however, I show how the increased policing has compelled many refugees to use digital technology more effectively, pushing individuals to take matters into their own hands, thereby evading both border guards and human smugglers. As I illustrate, digital technologies have had a transformational impact on clandestine migration, empowering migrants and refugees vis-à-vis smugglers and state authorities alike, allowing both groups to plan their own journeys, to stay in contact with family and friends both in the sending and receiving countries, and to seek assistance from peers who have previously made these crossings. As Rianne Dekker and Godfried Engbersen have argued (2012), the use of digital technology has democratized migration. Here I illustrate how the internet, social media, and smartphones have empowered migrants, allowing them to control their own journeys, to plan and document them and, in the process, to seize power back from the very smugglers upon whom they previously depended. Interestingly, however, the same digital technology has also allowed refugees to evade law enforcement officials on the border, permitting them to evade the European asylum process, including the EU-Turkey Agreement. In this final section, I briefly account the way in which this final unintended consequence occurs.

Democratizing Migration: The Use of Technology

Using free apps such as WhatsApp Messenger, Viber, Skype, Facebook, and other messaging tools, migrants are now able to communicate for free with family members and friends back home or in their destination countries, sending and receiving information and advice privately with others who have already made or who wish to make the journey clandestinely. The most popular of these messaging apps, WhatsApp Messenger, allows users to exchange messages without having to pay for SMS because it uses the same internet data plan that is used for email and web browsing; it also allows users to message across different platforms, to create groups, and to send each other unlimited photos, video, and audio messages. Voice mails and voice notes are also being widely used to facilitate communication.

In these ways, refugees are using the internet to navigate their own paths to northern Europe, stopping along the way at internet cafes, grocery stores, or anywhere they can access WiFi to make the necessary connections. By using such apps, they share and receive information about border crossings, clandestine paths, smugglers, and even the relative costs of trips, including discount offers. Dozens of private Facebook groups like "Asylum and Immigration Without Smugglers," "Asylum and Migration in all Europe," "Bus Stop for the Lost Ones," and "Asylum in Sweden, Holland, Norway, Germany, Britain, Austria, and Switzerland" are among the groups that have been created to help refugees enter Europe clandestinely. A prominent example is "Asylum and Immigration Without Smugglers," which had over 60,000 members in the summer of 2015 and which functions much like TripAdvisor, providing Syrian and other refugees with information on refugee-friendly hostels and hotels, the trustworthiness of specific smugglers, sea, and weather conditions, annotated maps, and even information on European bureaucracy and asylum law, such as where and how refugees must register with local authorities in different states of the European Union and where to find social services. A typical post on this site reads: "The sea today and tomorrow is fatally dangerous. Don't underestimate the situation. We have enough victims." Days later, the site instructs, "The storm is practically over. The best island to leave for today is Mytilene (Lesbos)" (quoted in Schmidle 2015).

Refugees also use WhatsApp to update their location on Google Maps. Interestingly, this is done often to alert the Greek coast guard of their location once in Greek waters so as to be met upon arrival onshore or to be rescued at sea in case of an accident. Google Maps is also used by refugees and other migrants to help them navigate their way across Europe, including information on border crossings. As a result of such applications, the level of control refugees have over their own migration continues to increase. For example, the sharing of exact GPS coordinates permits others to follow in their footsteps, allowing them to make the trip without the assistance of smugglers and helping them evade border guards. The following examples of posts illustrate the manner in which peers can provide relevant information to each other:

> Guys, in which German federal state should I hand myself over to the police? Where will I get a residence permit the quickest?
>
> If I get residence in Germany, will I be allowed to travel to Lebanon?
>
> Quickly, quickly! I need a hotel in Belgrade, does anyone have any addresses?
>
> Guys, will $2,500 be enough? (quoted in Assir 2015)

Thus, in the words of one refugee, "On Facebook, we Syrians help each other and give each other advice" (quoted in Assir 2015). Joel Millman of the International Organization for Migration corroborates that when Syrians arrive in Italy or Greece "they just melt away at the pier—they get on Facebook, and they know where to go" (quoted in Schmidle 2015). Rey Rodrigues of the International Rescue Committee agrees that the use of technology by migrants "offers a small level of control during a time of great uncertainty" (quoted in Ram 2015).

In closing, it is interesting to note that, as European policy-makers are engaged in efforts to stop human smuggling in the Mediterranean and to project an image of control and closure, in the end it may be refugees themselves, through the use of digital technologies, who may put smugglers out of business. As demand for smuggling services declines, so will the supply of such services. As one observer argues, "By providing refugees with this kind of autonomy and peer review, social networks could alter the system on the ground, and render the services of those persons profiting off of refugees . . . unnecessary" (Ram 2015). This observation is confirmed by refugees themselves who argue that increasingly they need less assistance from human smugglers: "Right now, the traffickers are losing business because people are going alone, thanks to Facebook" (quoted in Brunwasser 2015). Indeed, because of peer-to-peer messaging, some smugglers have been put out of business. For others, smuggling has become less profitable as prices have reportedly declined. What this does to the image of border control, its concomitant policy, and any unintended consequences that result remains to be seen. What is unmistakably true, however, is that the face of European migration is changing—new challenges have created new (and, as I have argued, ineffective) policies as well as new responses by refugees and migrants using technology to adapt to this changing migration picture.

Notes

1. This article was first presented at the International Political Science Association 24th World Congress of Political Science in Poznan, Poland, from 23–28 July 2016. I would like to thank Marybeth Ulrich, who served as discussant on that panel and who provided valuable feedback which helped to improve this article. Thank you also to the Department of Political Science and the College of Arts and Sciences at Indiana University South Bend as well as to the Office of the Vice President of Overseas Affairs at Indiana University Bloomington which generously supported the presentation with travel funding.
2. While the Dublin Regulation required asylum seekers to be registered and fingerprinted in the first EU country entered, in Greece asylum seekers who registered with the police were given a six-month residency permit, preventing deportation, but also not requiring settlement in the country.
3. For every Syrian who did not apply for asylum or whose asylum claim was not approved in Greece and therefore returned to Turkey, a one-to-one exchange would occur, with Turkey sending another Syrian asylum seeker for relocation to Europe up to a maximum of 72,000 people. To obtain Turkey's cooperation in slowing the flow of clandestine crossings into Greece, the EU agreed to provide Turkey with €6 billion in aid, visa-free travel for Turkish citizens to the EU's Schengen Zone, and an acceleration of talks on Turkey's accession to the European Union.
4. Reportedly, Arabs or Africans work as salesmen or brokers, while Turks or men from the former Soviet Union do the actual smuggling work across the Mediterranean.
5. Many women also reported similar exploitation faced at the hands of taxi drivers, hoteliers, and even European security staff at reception centers and border crossings.
6. This would include the Frontex personnel, who have been charged with conducting the initial screening and fingerprinting of asylum seekers in collaboration with the Greek police.
7. Some reports indicate that people wait in line for as much as five or more hours to receive their daily food rations.
8. A second group that is particularly prone to abuse and exploitation are the 22,000 migrant children currently in Greece and particularly the one-tenth of them who are unaccompanied or have been separated from their families.
9. To moderate some of the tensions between refugees in the camps, some detention centers have allowed refugees to come and go.
10. Afghans are feeling increasingly marginalized in the current process. This marginalization has come about as they are increasingly being reclassified as economic migrants rather than refugees.
11. Personal interview conducted by the author in Chios, Greece, June 28, 2016.
12. Personal interview conducted by the author in Chios, Greece, July 3, 2016.

References

Amnesty International. 2016. "Female Refugees Face Physical Assault, Exploitation and Sexual Harassment on Their Journey through Europe." January 18. Retrieved June 3, 2016 (www.amnesty.org/en/latest/news/2016/01/female-refugees-face-physical-assault-exploitation-and-sexual-harassment-on-their-journey-through-europe/).

Andreas, Peter. 2009. *Border Games: Policing the U.S.-Mexico Divide*. Ithaca, NY: Cornell University Press.

Assir, Serene. 2015. "WhatsApp and Viber Light Way to Europe for Syrian Refugees." *The Times of Israel*. Retrieved April 15, 2016 (www.timesofisrael.com/facebook-whatsapp-and-viber-light-way-to-europe-for-syrian-refugees/).

Brunwasser, Matthew. 2015. "A 21st-Century Migrant's Essentials: Food, Shelter, Smartphone." *New York Times*, August 25. Retrieved April 15, 2016 (www.nytimes.com/2015/08/26/world/europe/a-21st-century-migrants-checklist-water-shelter-smartphone.html?_r=0).

Cabot, Heath. 2014. *On the Doorstep of Europe: Asylum and Citizenship in Greece*. Philadelphia, PA: University of Pennsylvania Press.

Chan, Sewell. 2016. "Migration to Greece by the Aegean Sea Has Plummeted, U.N. Says." *New York Times*, July 8. Retrieved August 1, 2016 (www.nytimes.com/2016/07/09/world/europe/migrants-greece.html).

Cornelius, Wayne A. and Takeyuki Tsuda. 2004. "Controlling Immigration: The Limits of Government Intervention." Pp. 3–48 in Wayne A. Cornelius, Takeyuki Tsuda, Philip L. Martin, and James F. Hollifield, eds. *Controlling Immigration: A Global Perspective*. Stanford, CA: Stanford University Press.

Dekker, Rianne and Godfried Engbersen. 2012. "How Social Media Transform Migrant Networks and Faciliate Migration." *International Migration Institute Working Papers Series* 64(November).

DW. 2016. "More Than 3,000 Migrants Rescued at Sea in 72 Hours, Says Italian Coast Guard." *DeutscheWelle*, June 11. Retrieved June 12, 2016 (www.dw.com/en/more-than-3000-migrants-rescued-at-sea-in-72-hours-says-italian-coast-guard/a-19324025).

Guiraudon, Virginie and Christian Joppke, eds. 2001. *Controlling a New Migration World*. New York: Routledge.

Human Rights Watch. 2016. "Greece: Refugee 'Hotspots' Unsafe, Unsanitary: Women, Children Fearful, Unprotected; Lack Basic Shelter." May 19. Retrieved June 3, 2016 (www.hrw.org/news/2016/05/19/greece-refugee-hotspots-unsafe-unsanitary).

International Organization for Migration (IOM). 2016. "Europe/Migration Mediterranean Response: Situational Report." June 2. Retrieved June 12, 2016 (www.iom-nederland.nl/images/Nieuws/2016/februari/europe-mediterranean-migration-crisis-response-situation-report-02-june-2016.pdf).

Japan Times. 2016. "Migrants Take to Fields to Avoid State-Run Camps as Greece Ends Idomeni Sweep." *Japan Times*, May 27. Retrieved June 3, 2016 (www.japantimes.co.jp/news/2016/05/27/world/social-issues-world/migrants-take-fields-avoid-state-run-camps-greece-ends-idomeni-sweep/#.V04GeTa4Jn8/).

Joppke, Christian. 2004. "Commentary." Pp. 381–5 in Wayne A. Cornelius, Takeyuki Tsuda, Philip L. Martin, and James F. Hollifield, eds. *Controlling Immigration: A Global Perspective*. Stanford, CA: Stanford University Press.

Kingsley, Patrick. 2016. "More Than 700 Migrants Feared Dead in Three Mediterranean Sinkings." *The Guardian*, May 29. Retrieved June 4, 2016 (www.theguardian.com/world/2016/may/29/700-migrants-feared-dead-mediterranean-says-un-refugees).

Kosmopoulos, Giorgos. 2016. "Refugee Women on Greek Islands in Constant Fear." *News Deeply*, June 6. Retrieved June 12, 2016 (www.newsdeeply.com/refugees/op-eds/2016/06/06/refugee-women-on-greek-islands-in-constant-fear).

Lamb, Ismini A. 2016. "The Gates of Greece: Refugees and Policy Choices." *Mediterranean Quarterly* 27(2):67–88.

Lopez, Oscar. 2016. "E.U. Politics Turn Migrants' Dreams Into Nightmares on an Overcrowded Greek Island." *Time.com*, April 13. Retrieved April 17, 2016 (http://time.com/4292323/chios-greece-island-refugees/).

Margaronis, Maria. 2016. "The EU Has Turned Greece Into a Prison for Refugees." *The Nation*, May 27. Retrieved June 4, 2016 (www.thenation.com/article/the-eu-has-turned-greece-into-a-prison-for-refugees/).

Pazianou, Anthi. 2016. "Syrian Migrant Wins Appeal in Greece against Deportation to Turkey: Lawyer." *Xinhua*, May 29. Retrieved June 3, 2016 (http://news.xinhuanet.com/english/2016-05/29/c_135397072.htm).

Personal Interview. 2016. Conducted in Chios, Greece, by the author (June 28).

Personal Interview. 2016. Conducted in Chios, Greece, by the author (July 3).

Ram, Alessandra. 2015. "Smartphones Bring Solace and Aid to Desperate Refugees." *Wired.com*, December 5. Retrieved June 12, 2016 (www.wired.com/2015/12/smartphone-syrian-refugee-crisis/).

Schmidle, Nicholas. 2015. "Ten Borders: One Refugee's Epic Escape from Syria." *The New Yorker*, October 26. Retrieved June 12, 2016 (www.newyorker.com/magazine/2015/10/26/ten-borders).

Squires, Nick. 2016. "Migrants on Greece-Macedonia Border Refuse to Give Up Hope Despite EU-Turkey Deal." *The Telegraph*, March 18. Retrieved April 15, 2016 (www.telegraph.co.uk/news/worldnews/europe/greece/12198057/Migrants-on-Greece-Macedonia-border-refuse-to-give-up-hope-despite-EU-Turkey-deal.html).

Tomic, Lidija. 2016. "'Idomeni' Springs up on Serbian-Hungarian Border." *Deutsche Welle*, May 31. Retrieved June 4, 2016 (www.dw.com/en/idomeni-springs-up-on-serbian-hungarian-border/a-19295010).

Townsend, Mark. 2016. "Protests Grow as Greece Moves Refugees to Warehouses 'Not Fit for Animals'." *The Guardian*, May 28. Retrieved June 12, 2016 (www.theguardian.com/world/2016/may/28/greece-refugee-warehouses-not-fit-for-animals).

Trafford, Robert. 2016. "The Chios Hilton: Inside the Refugee Camp That Makes Prison Look Like a Five-Star Hotel." *The Independent*, April 22. Retrieved June 4, 2016 (www.independent.co.uk/news/world/europe/the-chios-hilton-inside-the-refugee-camp-that-makes-prison-look-like-a-five-star-hotel-a6996161.html).

Various Authors. 2016. "Letter to the Nobel Peace Prize Committee." January. Made available to the author by Elektra Kostopoulou.

Webb, Oscar. 2016. "Locals Throw Fireworks and Bottles at Migrants to Demand They Leave Greek Island of Chios." *The Telegraph*, April 8. Retrieved April 16, 2016 (www.telegraph.co.uk/news/2016/04/08/locals-throw-fireworks-and-bottles-at-migrants-to-demand-they-le/).

PGMO 08/21/2018